BUTTERCREAM
Palette Knife Painting Techniques

A Comprehensive Guide to Textured Art Using Buttercream Icing

Valeri Valeriano and Christina Ong

www.queenofheartscouturecakes.com

Contents

CAKE BASICS

Equipment	6
Colouring	7
Buttercream Recipes	8
Cake Recipes	13
Stacking & Dowelling	14
Crumb Coating	16
Smoothing	17
Marbling	18
Basic Strokes	20

BACKGROUNDS & PATTERNS

Sweet Stipple	30
Soft Florals	32
Geometric Tiles	34
Marvellous Mountains	36
Gold Leaf Marble	38
Pretty Patches	40
Scenic Landscape	42
Sunrise Over the Ocean	44
Fun Floral Dots	46
Exquisite Tiles	48
Stunning Spades	50
Groovy Shells	52

IMPRESSIONIST STYLE

Freehand Fleurs	56
Shades of Fall	58
Fresh Fruit Basket	62
Mysterious Maiden	66
Scarlet the Parrot	70

2 DIMENSIONAL TECHNIQUES

Leaves & Ferns	76
Fillers & Wildflowers	77
2D Flowers	78
Summer Garden	106
Floral Symphony	108
Beautiful Blooms	110
Rose Soiree	112

3 DIMENSIONAL TECHNIQUES

Sunflower	116
Lotus	118
Dogwood	120
Hydrangea	122
Peony	124
Orchid	128
Iris	130
Floral Reverie	134

Templates	138
About the Authors	140
Acknowledgements	
Index	141

Introduction

The world of cake decorating has evolved so much over the years. Today, inspiration comes from every source of beauty and style: art, nature, fashion, and more. In delicious buttercream frosting, cake decorators like you recreate lovely flowers, scenery, abstract designs, and other elements that make a delicious impact.

You do not need an artistic background to make impressive desserts. We come from a medical background with no advanced training in cake decorating at all. Over the years, we have experimented, learned, and now innovated unique palette knife painting techniques that allow anyone to decorate like a pro. All you need is creative vision, simple tools, rich buttercream recipe, the drive to learn, and this book.

Any design can translate into a palette knife painting design. Here you will learn different applications, strokes, and techniques to create anything. Make attractive backgrounds, floral elements, impressionist paintings, accents, and more for any size and shape cake. From the simplest design to the most complex imagery, you can find everything in this book.

We have been teaching palette knife painting for more than a decade now. This book builds on the basic instructions found in our previous publications. Our goal is to make this style of cake decorating with delicious buttercream frosting truly accessible to everyone. We have made sure to include as many applications as possible so you can use this technique in creating lovely textured backgrounds, floal designs, impressionist style art, sculptured elements and so much more.

Join us and explore a new world of palette knife painting techniques that will help you unlock your own creativity and discover new abilities in the field of cake decorating.

Happy BUTTERCREAM palette knife painting!

Cake Basics

Understanding the basics empowers you to create delicious, visually appealing cakes, troubleshoot issues, and explore your creativity. In essence, cake basics are fundamental for successful, enjoyable cake baking and decoration, whether for personal or professional purposes.

& Essentials

By mastering these fundamental cake decorating skills, you'll have a strong foundation to create a wide range of beautifully decorated cakes, from simple designs to more complex and elaborate creations.

Equipment

Colouring

Colours can simply transform a plain dessert into a vibrant and eye-catching masterpiece. The use of colours allows for endless possibilities in terms of design, patterns and themes, making your baked goods more attractive and engaging.

In essence, tinting buttercream adds an artistic dimension to baking and cake decorating. It allows bakers to go beyond just taste and texture, creating desserts that are visually captivating and memorable. It's a way to showcase your artistic talents and experiment with different colour combinations, shades, and techniques. When creating multi-layered cakes or desserts with various components, tinted buttercream helps maintain a coordinated and harmonious design. You can use the same colour palette throughout the dessert to tie everything together visually.

We have highlighted below the things you should remember when mixing colours.

- It is easier to tint your buttercream if it is at room temperature. Regulate the amount of gel colour that you add as it is really easy to overdo it.
- Mix it manually using your spatula if you are tinting a small batch. Smear the colour across the surface of the buttercream, then scoop and fold. Repeat the same process until it is even. For bigger batch, you may use your mixer but do it in the slowest speed possible.
- Buttercream naturally heightens its colour after a while, so do make sure to tint your buttercream at least 2 shades lighter when preparing. Prepare your buttercream ahead of time to have an allowance for colour change.
- Buttercream can be a bit yellowish, to make it slightly lighter, you may add a very tiny amount of violet gel colour. But to make it white, you will have to use a whitener colour.
- For big cake projects, make sure you prepare enough tinted buttercream. It is difficult, if not impossible to create the exact same colour if you need more.
- Use less colouring for light colours and add more for dark colours.
- To create a red colour, use a mixture of red, pink and orange. You may add a hint of brown or black to make it really dark.
- To create a black colour, tint your buttercream with any dark colour first then add the black colouring afterwards. This will prevent you from using too much of the black colour.
- If you think that you are going to use a lot of gel colouring, do not add the water initially when you prepare your buttercream as this may result in your buttercream to become too soft.
- You may use the "microwave method" to deepen the darkness of your buttercream. Do it in 3 seconds burst until it becomes really dark. Put it back in the fridge to retrieve the buttercream's original consistency.

- You may use brown to tone down the brightness of any colour. Add a small amount. A little too much might ruin the entire batch.
- If you accidentally make it too dark, add more plain buttercream. If it's too light, add more colouring.
- Practice combining two or three colours to create a more specific colour. Example, mix pink and orange to create a salmon colour. Pink and brown to create a chestnut colour and so on.
- If you only have powder colours to use, turn it into a paste mixture first by adding a small amount of water. Using the powder straight on to your buttercream may result to dark speckles formed into the buttercream.
- Different brands of colours will have different level of strength and concentration. Always try a small amount first to avoid wasting your buttercream.

Buttercream Recipes

QoHCC Buttercream

Never over-beat your buttercream. If you do, it will become grainy, and the edges are more likely to break or separate when you create textures and accents like flowers. When you over-beat, you incorporate a lot of air into the frosting. The surface will show these bubbles or air pockets and make smoothing it out very difficult. A stand mixer helps prevent this. If you use a hand mixer, fold the mixture manually first to incorporate the ingredients.

This recipe is quite flexible. You can add a little more or less of each ingredient to get the perfect consistency. Is the buttercream too stiff? Add a bit of water or milk. Is it too thin? Add more sugar. Use the frosting right away or refrigerate it for about an hour until it gets harder.

You will need

- 225g (8oz) butter, room temperature
- 115g (4oz) medium soft vegetable fat (shortening) (Trex), at room temperature, OR 225g (8oz) of soft spreadable vegetable fat (shortening) (Crisco)
- 600g (1lb 5oz) icing sugar (confectioners' sugar). sifted, if using medium soft vegetable fat (shortening) OR 750g (1lb 10oz) icing sugar (confectioners' sugar). sifted, if using soft spreadable vegetable fat (shortening)
- 2-3 tsp vanilla essence, or your choice of flavouring
- 1 tbsp water or milk (omit if you live in a hot country or whenever the temperature is hot)
- Mixer (hand-held or stand mixer)
- Mixing bowls
- Spatula
- Sieve (sifter/strainer)
- Measuring spoons

1. Beat the butter at medium speed until soft and pale (about 1 to 2 minutes). Some brands of butter are more yellow in colour, so to make it paler you can increase the beating time to about 2 to 5 minutes.

2. Add the vegetable fat (shortening) and beat for another 20 to 30 seconds or less. Make sure that it is well incorporated and that there are no lumps.

Important note: As soon as you add anything to the butter, you must limit your beating time to 20 to 30 seconds or even less.

3. Add vanilla essence, or your flavour of choice, and water or milk, then beat at medium speed for about 10 to 20 seconds until well incorporated

4. Slowly add the sifted icing sugar (confectioners' sugar) and beat at medium speed for another 20 to 30 seconds or until everything is combined. You may want to fold the ingredients together manually before beating to avoid puffing clouds of sugar round your kitchen.

Make sure you scrape the sides and bottom of your bowl, as well as the blade of your mixer, so you don't miss any lumps of icing sugar.

5. Lastly, after scraping the bowl, beat again for about 20 to 30 seconds and do not over-mix. This yields a perfect piping consistency of buttercream.

It is normal for the buttercream to have a somewhat grainy texture when it is first made because you are merely combining the ingredients, and not cooking or dissolving the icing sugar (confectioners' sugar) to turn the mix into a liquid. To improve the texture, completely melt the vegetable fat (shortening) and leave it to cool before adding it to your beaten butter, then proceed as normal. After making the buttercream this way, it will look like it is curdled. Do not panic! This is also normal!

Let it sit in your kitchen at room temperature for about 1 to 2 hours to allow the powdered sugar to slightly dissolve into the vegetable fat (shortening) and butter mixture. Then chill the buttercream in the fridge for a few hours or until firm. Allow enough time for the thawing process. Use a spatula and mix it manually, massage your piping bag to soften the buttercream or you may beat it under a sand mixer atthe lowest speed.

Vegetable Fat

This white, solid fat is made from flavourless vegetable oils. It is commonly sold near butter and margarines in grocery stores. Despite the name buttercream, our recipe uses vegetable shortening to create a more stable consistency that will hold up over time and in different conditions. This also reduces the amount of icing sugar (confectioners' sugar) you have to add, which prevents overbearing sweetness. Using this ingredient also helps the surface of your cake to form a crust so you can easily smoothen it out (see cake covering/smoothing).

Different brands of vegetable shortening have different consistencies. If you use a variety that is too hard, soften it for several seconds in the microwave before blending it with other ingredients. Also, adjust the amount of shortening in the recipe depending on the consistency. Trex brand is medium-hard, for example, so you can use 4 ounces (115g) Crisco, which is very soft and spreadable, would need double the amount for the same result.

Adding Flavours

Flavoured buttercream frosting adds character to your cake. There are many options to choose from including cocoa powder, fruit jams, squashed berries, peanut butter, or commercially prepared confectionery flavours. Always pay attention to the consistency. Follow the buttercream frosting recipe first and then add the flavours afterward. If it is too soft, add more icing sugar to the mix. You can also reduce the amount of water or other liquid ingredients.

Coverage

One basic buttercream recipe will yield approximately 1 kg (2 lbs. 8 oz.) of frosting. This will cover the top and sides of a 20 cm (8 inch) round or square cake with some left over for in between two layers. This coverage estimation can help you determine how much of each ingredient to use for your project. You can store leftovers in the fridge.

PRO TIP:

- We suggest to use soft unsalted butter.
- Beat or stir vegetable shortening first to make it smooth and get rid of any lumps.
- Do not use vanilla bean paste with seeds to avoid tiny black spots in the frosting.
- For hot and humid climates, omit the water in the recipe and only added gradually in the end to get the right consistency.
- Always sift your icing sugar.
- Use the paddle attachment on a stand mixer instead of the whisk attachment.Do not overbeat the recipe. Only do it enough to mix the ingredients fully together.

- If you do overbeat the buttercream, chill it first or freeze it then massage the bag of frosting or use a handheld spatula to mix it again.
- Store buttercream in resealable bags for up to 14 days in the refrigerator or a month in the freezer.
- If removing from the fridge or freezer, thaw the buttercream first. Ideally, just massage it manually using a handheld spatula to smooth it out or beat it with a stand mixer with a paddle attachment at the lowest speed possible. Do this for 30 seconds or less.
- Add in extra flavour ingredients at the very end.

Italian Meringue Buttercream

Italian meringue is quite similar to the Swiss version. It is delicious, light, silky, and creamy. This buttercream type is more stable than SMBC (Swiss Meringue Buttercream) due to the inclusion of hot sugar syrup. Preparing it takes a little longer, however, the output is totally worth it.

You will need

- 5 or 6 large egg whites
- 375g (13oz) granulated sugar
- 180ml (6¼fl oz) water
- 550g (1lb 4oz) unsalted butter, at room temperature
- 200g (7oz) solid vegetable fat (shortening), at room temperature (optional, makes it stable)
- 2 tbsp vanilla extract
- Pinch of salt and/or cream of tartar (optional)

1. In a large heavy-bottomed saucepan, mix half the sugar with the water over medium heat and stir until the sugar dissolves. Brush around the sides of the pan with a clean pastry brush dipped in water to dissolve any sugar crystals - you don't want the sugar to burn on the pan sides.

2. Attach a sugar thermometer to the side of the pan and continue boiling without stirring, until the sugar solution reaches 110°C (225°F).

3. Meanwhile, whisk the egg whites and remaining sugar in a stand mixer on low speed until the sugar is slightly dissolved. You can add a pinch of salt and/or cream of tartar for stability if you wish.

4. Once the egg whites are starting to become white in colour and forming stiff peaks, turn your mixer up to high and slowly pour the sugar syrup down the side of the bowl. Avoid splashing the syrup onto the whisk attachment so as not to make spun sugar.

5. Continue whipping the whites until the mixture has cooled down. The bottom of the bowl should feel barely warm.

6. Switch to the paddle attachment. Once the meringue is cool to touch, slowly add the butter/vegetable fat (shortening), which should be at room temperature, while beating at medium-high speed. Then slowly add the vanilla extract.

7. When the mixture is well blended and smooth, and when there are no remaining pieces of butter, you can stop or switch to the whisk attachment on low-medium speed to make the buttercream fluffy.

8. Once the meringue is cool to touch, slowly add the butter that is at room temperature while beating at medium to high speed.

9. When the buttercream has already formed a structure, add the vanilla and a pinch of salt. Continue mixing until well incorporated.

PRO TIP:

- Add flavor extracts, such as vanilla or almond, after the butter has been fully incorporated. This prevents over-mixing, which can cause the buttercream to become too soft.
- Make sure the whipped egg whites are at room temperature before adding the butter. If they're still warm, the butter could melt and result in a runny frosting.
- Once the buttercream is fully mixed, check its consistency. If it's too soft, place it in the refrigerator for about 15-20 minutes, then re-whip until smooth.
- Italian meringue buttercream can be stored in an airtight container in the refrigerator for up to a week or in the freezer for several months. Before using, allow it to come to room temperature and re-whip it for a smooth texture.

Swiss Meringue Buttercream

If you want a light and creamy buttercream frosting, Swiss meringue buttercream is your best option. It tastes delicious and looks beautiful with a distinct mousse like texture. It is silky smooth and pipes like a dream. This frosting may be a bit time-consuming to prepare when you begin but will quickly become second nature if you use it frequently for your cakes. This type of buttercream does not form a crust, but it holds its shape just fine.

You will need

- 5 large egg whites
- 250g (9oz) granulated sugar
- 340g (11¾oz) unsalted butter, cubed and at room temperature
- 2 tsp vanilla
- ¼ tsp salt

1. Make a bain-marie (double boiler) by placing a bowl over a saucepan of simmering water, making sure the bowl doesn't touch the water.

2. Add the egg whites and sugar to the bowl, whisking constantly but gently, until temperature reaches 60°C (140°F), or until the sugar has completely dissolved and the egg whites are hot to touch.

3. Remove from the heat and pour into the bowl of a stand mixer with the whisk attachment and begin to whip until the meringue is thick, glossy, and the bottom of the bowl no longer feels warm - about 7 to 10 minutes.

4. Switch to the paddle attachment and, with mixer on low speed, add the butter cubes one at a time until incorporated. Continue beating until the mixture has a silky-smooth texture. If the buttercream curdles, simply keep mixing and it will come back to smooth. If the buttercream is too thin and runny, refrigerate it for about 15 minutes before continuing to mix it with the paddle attachment until it comes together. Add the vanilla and salt, continuing to beat on low speed until well combined.

• •

Bean Paste Buttercream   (Vegan Option)

This recipe is made with a puréed soft bean base. Bring it to a simmer until the water is evaporated to create the paste that works well as a vegan alternative to buttercream. This is also a great option for those who want healthier desserts.

You will need

- 500g (1lb 2oz) any white beans (or you can also try raw cashew)
- 250g (9oz) sugar (you can lessen this amount as you prefer)
- ½ tsp salt
- 5 or 6 cups water

1. Rinse the white beans in cold water and soak until the beans are soft and double in size - for about 5 to 6 hours or overnight in the fridge.

2. Peel off the skin and drain the water.

3. Simmer the soaked white beans in 5 cups of water and add ½ tsp of salt over a high heat. Reduce the heat to medium and cook until copletely soft. Skim off any foam that comes up to the surface. If necessary, add more water. When the water is at the level of the beans, remove the pan from the heat and cool to room temperature.

4. Use a blender to puree the bean mixture. This will yield a very runny consistency.

5. Heat the smooth white bean paste in a clean pan over medium heat. Add all the sugar and stir to mix. As the paste is heated and the sugar is dissolved, the paste will become loose. Stir with a wooden spoon so that steam bubbles out and the paste thickens again. Taste and adjust the sweetness by adding more sugar as you desire.

6. Turn off the heat. Let the mixture cool completely and keep it in an airtight container. If you will be using it within three days, keep it refrigerated, otherwise, keep it frozen. You can defrost the paste by moving it to the fridge the night before you need it.

If the frosting seems too thick, you can add water, milk or cream, 1 tablespoon at a time, and mix until you achieve the desired consistency. Be careful not to add too much liquid, as it can make the buttercream too runny.

White Chocolate Ganache

Ratios in recipes refer to how much of one ingredient you mix with another. A common one for white chocolate ganache is 3:1 or three to one. This makes recipes scalable for different size cakes.

When making white chocolate ganache, we also use a 3:1 ratio as the result is creamy but firm enough for sculpture palette knife techniques. That would equate to 3 pounds of white chocolate to 1 pound of cream. Hotter climates may need to bump this up to 4:1. Real chocolate is firmer than candy melts. Use the same type and brand of white chocolate throughout for consistency.

You will need

- 600grams (21oz) white chocolate
- 200grams (7oz) whipping cream

1. Soften chocolate using bain-marie (double boiler) (see Swiss Meringue Buttercream) or the microwave method: You can do 10-second bursts and stirring to avoid chocolate from burning.

2. Simmer heavy whipping cream either over the stove or microwave method.

3. Pour the cream over the chocolate and gently stir using your spatula to incorporate the ingredients.

4. Pour the mixture into a shallow pan to cool and stiffen. Stir this until it is creamy and smooth. If the white chocolate ganache stiffens too much, put it in the microwave for several seconds before stirring it again.

... Colouring Tip ...

Adding concentrated food colouring to white chocolate ganache will not cause it to seize or change consistency. Simply add in a few drops at a time while stirring to create the desired colour. Oil-based colours create more vibrant and darker shades.

Cake Recipes

Vanilla Cake

This is our take on classic vanilla cake. The delicious, moist texture will stay fresh for up to five days. It goes well with any kind of frosting and is easy to work with and decorate.

You will need

- 300 grams (10.5oz) All purpose flour
- 1 tsp baking powder
- 1 tsp baking soda
- 1 tsp salt
- 300 (10.5) grams caster sugar (can be reduced to 250gms or 8.8oz)
- 1 block/ 2 sticks/ 225g unsalted butter
- 2 large eggs
- 2 tsps vanilla extract
- 250 ml or 1 cup buttermilk

1. Preheat the oven at 160C or 320F.

2. Sift the flour, baking powder, baking soda and salt.

3. Cream the butter for about 1-2 minutes. Add in the caster sugar. Cream them together for another 2mins.

4. Add both eggs and vanilla. Mix them together until well incorporated. Pour the rest of the sifted dry ingredients and the buttermilk. Mix until well incorporated.

5. Pour the batter in an 8x4in round pan (or 2pcs 8X2 round pans). Make sure that the pan/s has been applied with cake release mixture. Wrap the soaked baking strips.

6. Place your baking pan in the middle part of the oven, make sure that there is an oven thermometer for more accurate temperature. Bake for about 45-60mins. Insert a skewer to check if it is done.

Chocolate Cake

Out of the wide variety of cake flavours in the world, chocolate cake remains a favourite. Our cake recipe gives you a soft, moist, and is simply irresistible cake.

You will need

- 220 grams all-purpose flour
- 80 grams cocoa powder
- 1 tsp baking soda
- 1 tsp baking powder
- 1 tsp salt
- 300 grams caster sugar (can be reduced to 250gms)
- 225 grams soft, unsalted butter
- 2 pcs large eggs
- 1 cup room temperature milk
- 1 tsp vanilla extract
- 1 cup boiling water
- 1-2 tsps coffee dissolved in 2-3 tbsp hot water (optional)

1. Preheat the oven at 160C or 320F.

2. Sift the flour, cocoa powder, baking powder, baking soda and salt.

3. Cream the butter for about 1-2 minutes. Add in the caster sugar. Cream them together for another 2mins.

4. Add both eggs and vanilla. Mix them together until well incorporated. Pour the rest of the sifted dry ingredients and the milk. Mix until well incorporated.

5. Pour the boiling water (with optional 1-2 tsps coffee). Start mixing in slow speed until slightly incorporated then mix in medium speed.

6. Pour the batter in an 8x4in round pan (or 2pcs 8X2 round pans). Make sure that the pan/s has been applied with cake release mixture.

7. Place your baking pan in the middle part of the oven, make sure that there is an oven thermometer for more accurate temperature.

8. Bake for about 60-70 mins. Insert a skewer to check if it is done.

Cake Basics

Stacking and Dowelling

Taller cakes need structure to support the upper layers so that they will not collapse. This requires plastic or wooden dowels or even large plastic straws inserted into the lower levels. These help bear the weight of the above sections.

You do not need dowels for up to three cake layers. Any cakes with greater height will need them or you risk the whole thing collapsing or getting squashed.

You will need

- Four cake layers of your chosen size
- Three 1-2mm (1/16in) thin cake boards (not cake cards) that are sturdy but cuttable
- Cake drum
- Cake leveler or serrated knife
- Plastic or wooden dowels or straws
- Wire cutters or heavy-duty scissors
- Pencil or pen
- Non-toxic glue

PRO TIP:

To cut multiple dowels to the same correct length, push one into the base cake layer until it reaches the bottom. Draw a mark on the dowel at the top of the cake layer, remove it, and cut it at the mark. Use this as a measuring tool for the other dowels.

1. Trim the top surface of each cake layer with a leveler or serrated knife. Do this on a flat surface to make sure each cake sponges are leveled properly.

2. Cut thin cake boards up to 5mm-10mm (¼ -½ in) larger than the cake layer. The diameter depends on the thickness of the intended buttercream frosting. Consider using the baking tin as a template. Use non-toxic glue to affix two boards back-to-back with silver sides out. Drive a dowel through the center to make a guide hole for later multi-level construction. To know the absolute center of the board, cut out the same size diameter from a parchment paper then fold it in half twice. The center is where the folds intersect. Use that template as a guide later to know where to drive the central dowel in the latter process.

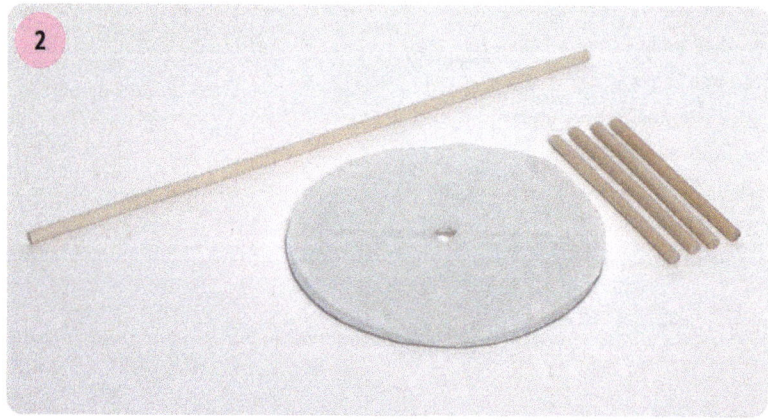

3. Place the first two cake layers on the remaining thin board, filling with desired frosting in between. Cut the dowels to this height.

4. Push the cut dowels into the bottom layer. These should be spaced evenly approximately 4cm or 1.5 inches away from the outer edge. Insert them until they reach the cake board at the bottom. The number used depends on the cake's size.

5. Cover protruding dowels with a thin layer of buttercream frosting then secure and stick the thin board to your main cake drum using non-toxic glue. Do not just use buttercream, ganache or royal icing as it could still slide about.

6. Repeat the above steps 3 and 4 and carefully stack the other two cake layers on top of the bottom combined cake layers.

7. Measure and cut the dowel which is the height of the whole cake.

8. Complete the dowelling process by inserting one dowel in the center. This should be the whole height of the cake and fit through the holes in the center of the cake boards.

STACKING AND DOWELLING | 15

Covering Cakes

Crumb Coating

Crumb coating is sealing the cake with a thin amount of buttercream to make sure that no cake crumbs will mix up and show on the surface of the final cover. Before you add any wonderful decoration, you should do your crumb coating to make sure that the buttercream will stick to the surface and provide a clean base.

It is a crucial step in cake decorating that helps ensure a clean, smooth, and professional-looking final result. While it may add an extra step to the cake decorating process, the benefits in terms of appearance and ease of decorating make it well worth the effort.

1. Apply a good amount of buttercream all around the cake with a firm pressure using a piping bag with a round nozzle or just simply snip off the tip. Regulate the amount of buttercream as you apply as you only need a thin layer.

2. We prefer to use the short-angled palette knife to spread the buttercream evenly throughout the cake. Make sure to tilt your palette knife from side to side as you glide your hand up and down when spreading the buttercream.

3. Depending on the final decoration or your preference, you can leave the cake as textured as it is or even out the surface with a cake scraper. Chill the cake in the fridge for 15 to 30 minutes or until the surface is firm to the touch.

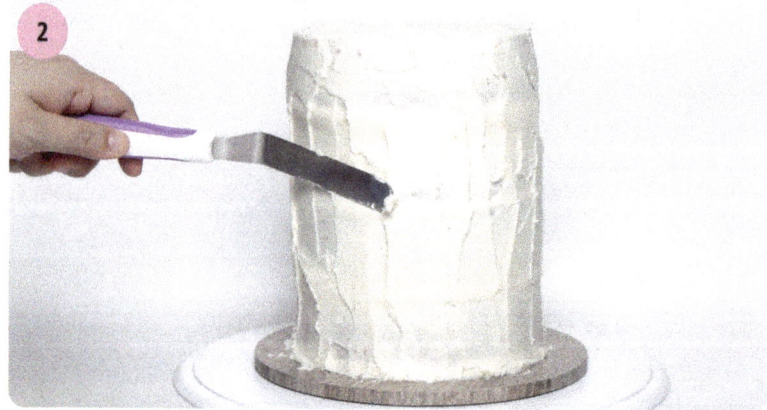

PRO TIP:

Before applying the crumb coat, make sure your cake is properly cooled. Ideally, it's best to bake the cake, let it cool completely, and then chill it in the refrigerator for about 20 to 30 minutes. A cold cake is easier to work with and less likely to crumble.

Smoothing

After chilling the cake sufficiently, you can now apply the final coating. Choose your desired thickness of the buttercream based on your tastes and decorating plan. If it is a single colour, use either plain buttercream or the same one for crumb coating. If you are using a blended or multi-coloured frosting, use plain, un-tinted frosting for this instead.

1. Spread the final coating of buttercream to the entire cake surface and spread it out with a palette knife until it is even.

2. Use a clean cake scraper to remove excess buttercream and make sure it has even thickness. Expect to see a few minor lines on the surface at this stage.

3. Use an offset spatula to smooth the buttercream on the top of the cake. Hold the spatula parallel to the surface for a clean finish.

4. Wait 5 or 10 minutes before continuing. This allows the buttercream to begin the drying process. Touch test it with a clean finger to check for a dry surface. It may feel slightly oily but the buttercream should not stick to your finger. When surface is dry, place your cake cloth gently on the surface and rub out any bumps or creases until the surface is level and smooth. Repeat this until the entire cake surface is done.

For additional smoothing, use the cake scraper over cake cloth again. Run it gently and repeatedly over the cloth to get rid of any remaining issues.

Finish the edges of the cake with a small palette knife or scraper. Use it to remove any excess buttercream that stands out after smoothing the surface. Let this part crust up again before repeating the cake cloth process.

Marbling

Blended Style

Marbled frosting is a beautiful and artistic way to decorate cakes and cupcakes. It involves creating swirls of two or more colours of frosting that resemble the patterns found in marble stone. This blended style gives a rather subtle marbled finish.

1. Apply the final coating of buttercream to the entire cake surface then even it out and remove any excess using a cake scraper.

2. Apply small dabs of your first marbling colour either by a piping bag with a small hole at the tip or directly with a palette palette knife.

3. Use a palette knife to swirl the first marbling colour to the background frosting. You can create various patterns, like loops, waves, or circular motions, to achieve the marbling effect.

4. Blend and even out the buttercream with short strokes moving repeatedly from left to right using a scraper. We prefer to use a bendy scraper so you have a better control.

5. Repeat the same process in step 2 and apply the other colour you want to marble.

6. Repeat the same technique in step 3 to further blend the colour to the background.

7. Repeat the same technique in step 4 to blend the buttercream.

8. If you want a more subtle marbled look, continue to even out the surface with a scraper. However, avoid over blending to maintain distinct color patterns.

It's a good idea to practice on a cake board before applying it to your cake. This way, you can experiment with different techniques and color combinations without affecting your final product.

Textured Style

Textured marbling refers to a decorative technique that combines the visual appeal of marbled patterns with a tactile or textured surface. This style creates raised or embossed elements that complement the marbled patterns. This effect pairs with all kinds of decorations.

1. Prepare your chosen colours and place them on a working board for ease of application.

2. Apply your final layer of buttercream with your chosen colour. Then load the back of your palette knife with a small amount of buttercream and lightly apply a very thin layer of frosting to the surface by gently gliding the palette knife across the surface of the cake in a random motion. This will create irregular textured surface.

3. Repeat the same process with short, controlled strokes. The goal is to apply a thin, broken layer of buttercream that partially covers the underlying layer. For added visual effect, allow some of the first layer to show through.

4. Choose your colours wisely as these will interact with the underlying layer to create a desired visual effect. Succeeding layers are often lighter in value than the underlying layer, but this can vary based on your intended outcome.

This technique gives a beautiful textured finsih that has a somewhat hazy effect. Depending on the colors used and the pressure applied, you can achieve effects like softening edges, adding a diffused glow, adjusting color temperature, or creating a sense of depth.

Remember that marbling can be a bit unpredictable, and each creation will be unique. Don't be afraid to experiment with different colors and techniques to achieve the look you desire.

MARBLING | 19

Basics Strokes

The basic strokes taught here give you a great foundation for cake decorating with a palette knife and piping bag accompaniment. Later on in the book, you will learn how to use them for a variety of different flowers and other buttercream designs. Keep in mind that you do not have to rigidly stick with a specific stroke for each flower or project. Once you learn the techniques, mix and match them and use the ones you are most comfortable with to get the finished look you want.

PIPING BAG METHOD

This basic stroke uses multiple tools to get the look you want. It represents the most beginner-friendly type of palette knife painting technique. Use a piping bag with your desired colour of buttercream with small to medium-sized tip.

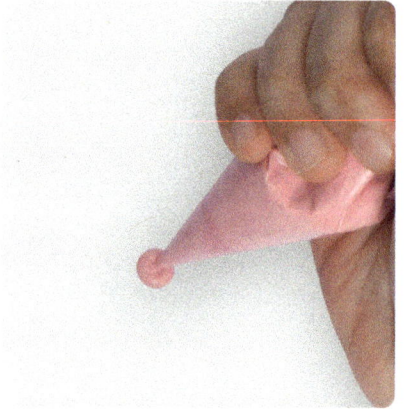

As the tip touches the surface, gently squeeze the piping bag to build a dot according to the size of the petal you require.

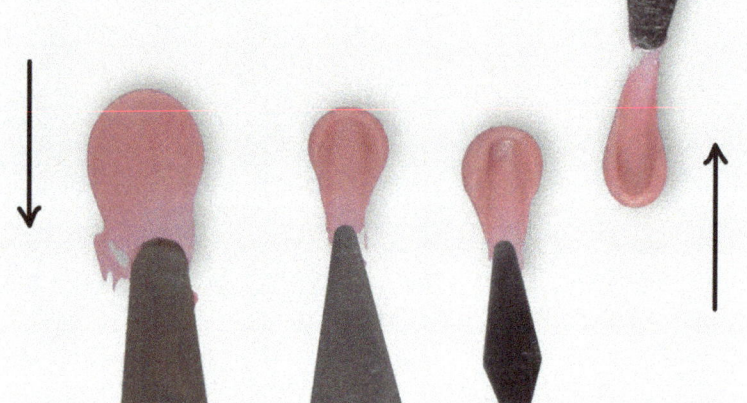

Switch to the right-sized palette knife for the effect you are trying to make. Use a wider blade for a completely flat design or a narrower one for a design with raised edges. The skinnier the blade, the more buttercream will remain on the edge.

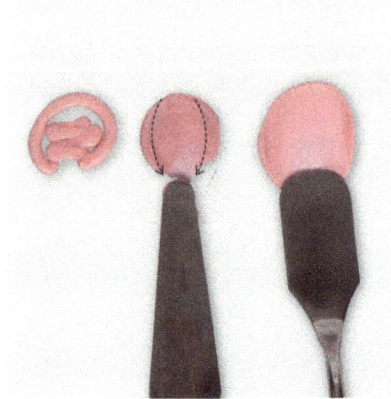
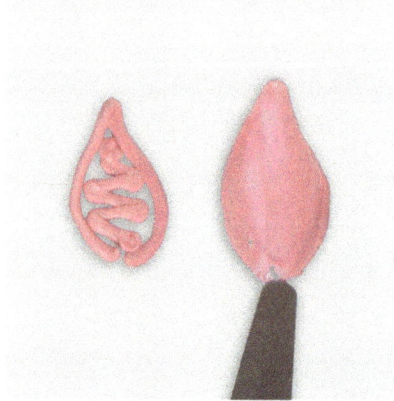

To achieve wider petals, instead of making a dot of buttercream with the piping bag, pipe a shape with the frosting instead. This can help you make larger elements or ones with more distinct angles or curves. Do not overfill the outline to prevent buttercream going where you do not want it to. Use your desired palette knife to spread this buttercream to create the final design. If it is very large or has multiple elements like petals or lobes on a leaf, work from the outside in to prevent any frosting going outside the outline. You can use multiple strokes if necessary.

PRESS & SLIDE

This common palette knife technique is used for a wide variety of designs. You can use different sizes and shapes of knife depending on the desired end result. Always keep the tip and the sides of the palette knife free of any excess buttercream to maintain neat and more precise shape of petals or any details.

Load the palette knife tip with an appropriate amount of buttercream frosting. Take care to use just enough for the petal, leaf, or other design you want to make. Smooth excess of the edges of the palette knife to prevent rough edges on the finished decoration.

Hold the knife blade almost perfectly flat against the surface. Press the buttercream down and then slide the knife blade while slowly lifting it from the surface to get the desired size and shape.

To create other shaped details or designs, use more buttercream frosting or different shaped palette knife. Press and slide with an even pressure to make an attractive shape without excess lumps, unevenness, or thin sections.

Avoid pressing too hard with the palette knife or you risk disturbing the frosting underneath or removing too much of the colour you are currently working with. Also, do not tilt the knife blade upward to prevent the tip gouging through the frosting and scraping the design. Keep the palette knife mostly flat against the surface of the cake.

PRESS & Curve

This palette knife technique is very similar to the press and slide option, but you move the knife to the side instead of straight in a line before picking it off the surface.

Load the back of the palette knife with a large amount of buttercream frosting. This should be appropriate for the size of the petal or other decorative element you intend to create. Do not overload it and especially for background elements like leaves or petals on the back edge of side-view flowers.

Slightly tilt the palette knife to the left to attach the frosting to the surface before sweeping it in a straight or curved motion to the right. This direction as seen in the photos suits right-handed individuals. If you are left-handed, you may do things in the opposite direction depending on the needs of the decorative design.

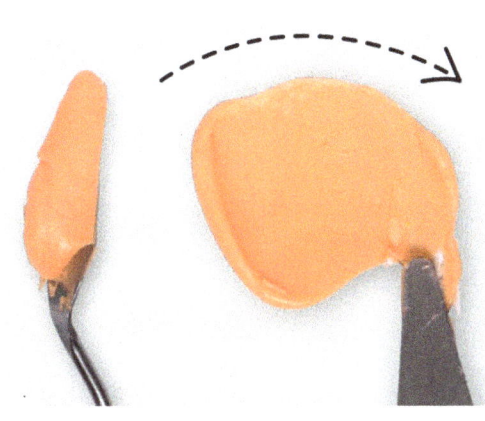

BASIC STROKES | 21

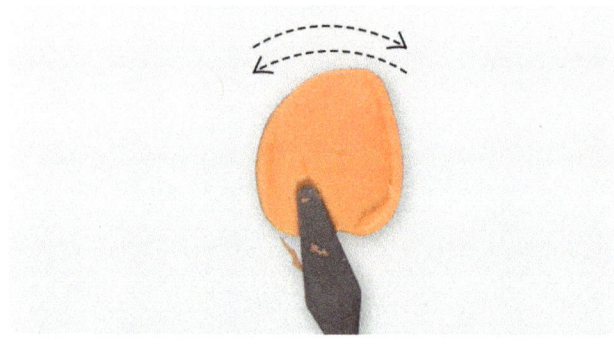 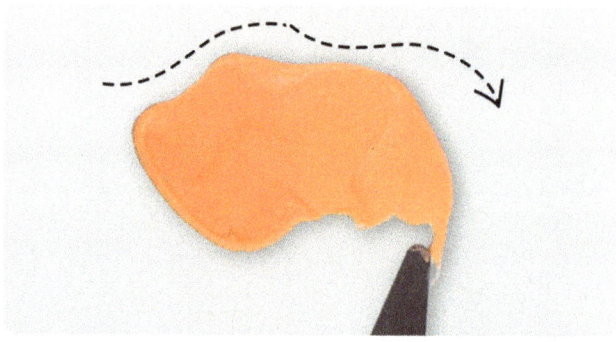

As you move the palette knife from the starting side to the endpoint or curved back and forth moton, decrease the angle so the buttercream frosting is smoothed over the surface appropriately. In most cases, you will finish the design with the palette knife blade parallel to the cake. Do not press too hard or you will risk scraping off lower layers or damaging the surface.

If the design is exceptionally wide or wavy in any way, load with more buttercream in the first step. This technique works much better if you have enough frosting available at the start. While gliding your hand from one side to the next, you can move your hand slightly up and down across the surface of the cake to create different edge effects.

PRESS & Curve with Rigid Movement

This palette knife technique is very similar to the press and curve option, but you move the knife further to the side picking it off the surface to create a wider petal.

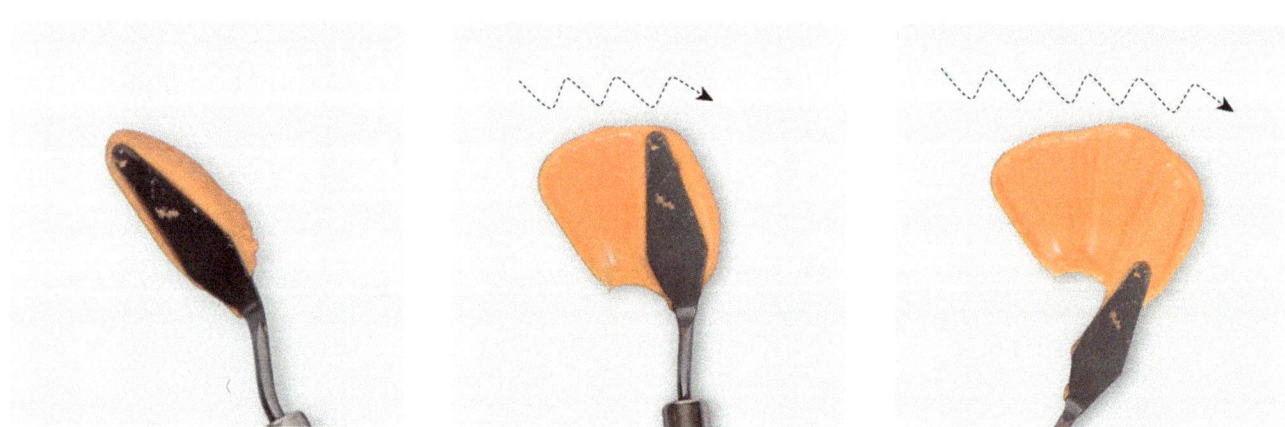

Load a sufficient amount of buttercream frosting onto your palette knife to complete the whole design.

As you glide the knife in a straight line or gentle curve to create the appropriate shape, use varying pressure with rigid and repeating up and down motion to apply the buttercream to the surface. You can do this in any height or width you prefer to get the look you want in the end. This will create a petal with lovely striated texture.

SIDE STROKE

Create broad flower petals or leaves using the side of the palette knife instead of the point or tip. This leaves a thicker edge at the top of the design that works very well for flowers with large petals and foreground elements.

Load your palette knife with a sufficient amount of buttercream frosting to complete each petal or leaf. Choose an appropriate knife with the right size blade to create each element. Hold the knife pointing to the side rather than straight ahead. Tilt the blade slightly to the side so you can glide the buttercream across the surface of the cake without pressing too hard or damaging any frosting below it. This also creates a lovely dimensional edge to the petal.

Slowly draw your knife down toward yourself while flattening the angle of the blade until it is parallel to the surface of the cake. Also increase pressure slightly to smooth out the application before pulling the knife away at the end.

This technique is especially useful for side facing flowers with petals that curve toward each other in the center. As you can see on the images, draw the palette knife gradually to the right or left as appropriate for the final design. You can also do so without curving the angle for the middle petals that overlap the ones on either side.

Here are some examples that used the SIDE STROKE technique:

BASIC STROKES | 23

Consistency

Buttercream frosting can be made in a variety of consistencies from very soft and spreadable to stiffer. The latter is more suitable for sculptural elements. You can see the difference in the images of the two styles of hydrangea flowers. The more three-dimensional the design, the stiffer the buttercream used. Another option is to use chocolate ganache. This allows you to create more detailed designs as well.

Adjust the consistency of the buttercream frosting by adding more or less liquid ingredients to the mix. This is also a good tip for locations with hotter temperatures or more humidity in the air. Stiffer frosting holds up better to weather conditions.

With palette knife painting, soft consistency frosting can increase the chance of colour bleed-through. Use thicker consistencies to prevent this or simply use a gentler touch and more frosting on top when layering colours.

Use of Palette Knives

Palette knives come in metal or plastic, and both work well for spreading buttercream over a cake. However, thinner, sturdier stainless steel often gives the best results in the most long-lasting way. They also come in a variety of sizes, widths, and angles. Having a whole set of different options helps you create more unique and beautiful decorative elements. Many flowers or other images use multiple palette knives to get the perfect look.

Ensure whatever decorative palette knives you choose have the appropriate angled handle. This keeps the handle and your fingers away from the cake surface while decorating. Finally, many of these knives come with numbers identifying the size or shape. We do not use these in our instructions. Instead, you will simply work according to the description of the tip – rounded or angled – the size – broad or narrow – and other specific details.

Understanding Angles

When decorating cakes, you use a variety of different angles with your palette knife to get the results you want. Covering the entire surface requires a relatively flat angle to use the maximum surface area of the knife. An example of this is the landscape cake shown here. More three-dimensional or sculptural elements use more severe angles to get the desired look.

This also affects whether you use the side of the knife or the tip alone. Your hand will naturally move in the right angle when using these different parts of the palette knife blade. Also, each decorative technique and element described in this book will be clearly described with the instructions.

In general, the flatter the finished cake decoration, the lower the knife angle. You will tilt the blade at more severe angles to create thicker or more detailed flowers as seen in the up-close image. This also allows you to apply higher volumes of buttercream frosting at the same time.

Layering & Detailing

The layering is a fundamental approach in painting. These beautiful layers will create depth, luminosity, and complexity in the artwork. You can do this with any medium you choose. Layering will allow you to gradually build up colors, values, and textures, resulting in a more realistic and visually appealing artwork.

Apply subsequent layers of your chosen medium as needed. In the final layers, you can refine details, adjust values, and enhance colors. Use smaller brushes or knives and more controlled strokes for this stage. Step back from time to time and review your artwork and make any necessary adjustments. Add final highlights, accents, and details to bring the painting to its desired level of completion.

Remember that the number of layers you use and the techniques you employ will vary depending on your artistic style, the medium you're using, and the specific effects you want to achieve. Be careful not to overdo the blending as this will lead to a loss of texture, vibrancy, and definition in the artwork.

Basic Strokes

While there are many different palette knife techniques and strokes described later on in this book, there are a few basic ideas that will help you get started. As you can see in these pictures, how you use the knife will directly affect the decorative outcome you get. You will often see words referring to how much pressure to use, whether to press hard or soft, and whether to make a stroke short or long, and wide or narrow.

You will understand more about the specific movements you make with your palette knife later on in the book. Knowing the basic strokes will help you create unique and beautiful designs that help the element come to life. For example, the impressionistic style in the fruit basket follows the basic form of the object you are creating. Other options will use different approaches.

Colour Palette

Choosing colours for your decorating design makes a huge difference for the impact of the finished cake. Use the classic artists colour wheel to choose shades that look good together. Get inspiration from nature, flower gardens, or your favourite art pieces.

When finding colours to use on the cake, consider things like complementary shades, monochromatic designs, and classic combinations that set specific moods. Complementary colours are those opposite each other on the colour wheel like orange and blue or yellow and purple. You can see this in the ocean-themed cake pictured here.

Monochromatic indicates shades that are closely related to a single colour. These stunning spades create a visually harmonious and cohesive look. Also, explore different color themes as they can evoke distinct feelings, emotions, mood and associations.

ESSENTIALS | 26

Composition

This term refers to the layout of the different elements that make up your overall design. We recommend that you draw it first on paper before you pick up your piping bag or palette knife. This helps ensure the design is well-balanced and will look good on the finished cake surface.

When decorating a cake, you start with the outermost or farthest away elements first. These are often leaves on a floral design like the one pictured here. Planning the composition helps you know where to begin so you do not end up trying to add in background bits and risk messing up the more prominent elements like the large flowers.

Use a piece of paper that is a similar size or dimension to the cake surface. Then, plan the composition to create a pleasing visual effect. Do not leave large empty spaces between elements like flowers, as that will look less natural and not as impressive. Overlapping flowers or other designs look better unless you are specifically making a scattered design on purpose.

Design Use

As you can see from the examples on this page, there are many different ways to use designs in cake decorating. You can create background textures with the simple stippling or tapping technique, smoother options like the multi-hued tiled cake, or painting effects like the lovely example of a colourful parrot. In this one, the design is used as the primary element itself.

There are so many different palette knife techniques and strokes to use. You do not have to use the same one across an entire cake nor do you need to use a specific technique every time you try a similar design. They can be used for backgrounds, two-dimensional images, sculptural elements, highlights and accents, and more. Planning the use of different techniques and designs before you begin can help create a more beautiful and impressive outcome.

Backgrounds

This chapter offers a variety of strokes, from broad and sweeping to fine and controlled, resulting in a dynamic visual impact. Consider the mood and style you want to convey. You can go for a limited colour palette or a more vibrant one. Imagination is the only limitation.

and Patterns

Use different techniques to create various textures, backgrounds and patterns – dragging, scraping, dabbing, stippling, layering and so much more. Experiment with different pressures and angles of the knife to achieve the desired effect.

Sweet Stipple

Create a beautiful velvety textured design on your cake with this palette knife technique. This is one of the easiest ways to spruce up the buttercream surface and present something beyond the ordinary. Learn how to create this stipple effect in just a few simple steps. Get your cake decorating palette knife ready and begin.

You will need

Tools:
- palette knife
- piping bags
- parchment paper squares 5cm (2in)
- Wilton petal nozzle 104
- Wilton petal nozzle 352

Cake:
- Round cake, 15cm (6in) X 10cm (4in) high

Buttercream:
- 200 gms (7oz) light pink for crumb coating
- 250 gms (8.8oz) light pink for final cover
- 100 gms (3.5oz) light pink
- 100 gms (3.5oz) extra light pink
- 100 gms (3.5oz) light green
- 60 gms (2.1oz) white

1. After piping over the base layer of buttercream with a colour design and filling in the spaces as desired, smooth this out with the edge of your palette knife. This should create a relatively flat surface to begin the blended tapping texture.

2. Turn the palette knife in your hand so the flat back faces the cake surface. Hold it parallel to prevent gouging out any of the frosting as you work around. Tap gently with the flat tip to create a velvety stipple effect. This should alternately indent and pull up small bits of frosting.

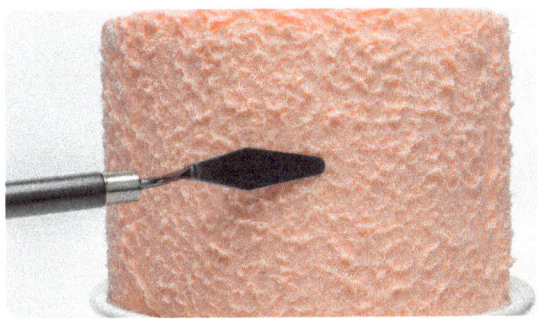

3. Repeat this process for the entire surface you want decorated with this unique texture. Be sure to overlap the tapping so there are no obvious lines or breaks in the stippling.

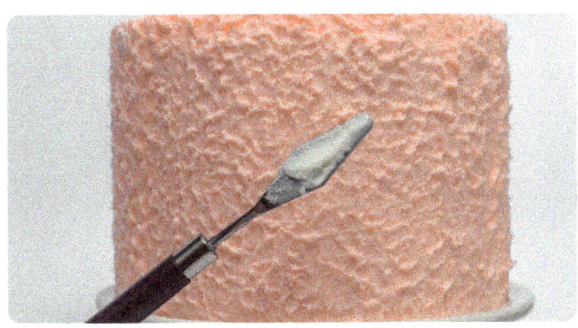

4. (Optional) Create a unique multi-color look by loading a clean palette knife with another shade of frosting.

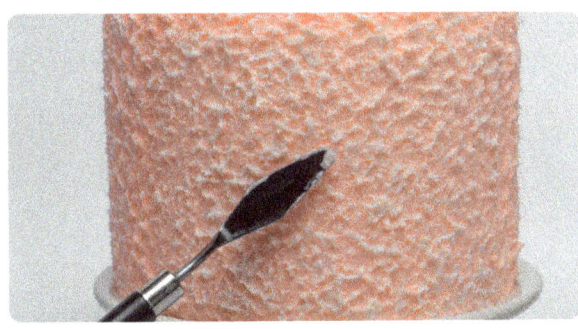

5. The example uses white for a delicate glow-up, but you can use your creativity to work with other color combinations. Repeat the tapping with a much gentler touch over the whole surface. Use very light pressure to apply color without flattening the texture.

 **PRO TIP:**

For larger cakes or frosting that dries more quickly, cover parts of the cake as you work around it. This will keep the buttercream at the right consistency for tapping.

Swiss meringue buttercream does not form a crust and is ideal for this technique.

Consider using this technique to create a shadowed effect or mimic the style of impressionist paintings and artwork.

The roses on this cake is optional. You can add some sugar or real flowers on your next project.

Soft Florals

Create a beautifully textured design on the sides of your cake to elevate ordinary artwork to something truly special. This palette knife technique is done by simply tapping the surface after filling and blending the coloured buttercream frosting. Try it with flowers, geometric shapes, or a simple swirl of lovely colour. The end result has a gentle dimensional stipple effect that softens the colours and designs of the original artwork.

You will need

Tools:
- palette knife
- piping bags

Cake:
- Round cake, 15cm (6in) X 15cm (6in) high

Buttercream:
- 500 gms (17.5oz) plain for crumb coating and final cover
- 80 gms (2.8oz) plain
- 80 gms (2.8oz) light green
- 80 gms (2.8oz) pale green
- 80 gms (2.8oz) dark pink
- 80 gms (2.8oz) dark violet
- 80 gms (2.8oz) dark orange

1. After applying the final cake cover, pipe over the base layer of buttercream with a coloured design and fill in the spaces as desired.

2. Gently blend and smooth this out with the edge of your palette knife. This should create a relatively flat surface to begin the tapping texture.

3. Repeat this process for the entire cake. You can work on individual design elements like flowers, buds and leaves.

4. Add additional base colour of frosting with a piping bag to ensure the surface is the same height/thickness all the way around the cake.

PRO TIP:

For larger cakes or frosting that dries more quickly, cover parts of the cake as you work around it. This will keep the buttercream at the right consistency for tapping.

Variation

Blend different colours as your background before doing the stippling. Add a splash of metallic paint for aesthetic.

5. Use a clean palette knife to gently tap over the entire surface of the cake frosting design. Use the tip of the knife held parallel to the surface of the cake. Be careful not to gouge dents into the frosting and keep the thickness the same all the way around. Finally, add some highlight or shadow effect on your elements as you go or simply move around the circumference.

SOFT FLORALS | 33

Geometric Tiles

Create a unique cake that mimics the amazing style of mosaic tiles or architectural plasterwork in delicious buttercream. This decorating design looks a lot more difficult than it truly is to create. Try your favourite colours or patterns to make a unique look every time.

You will need

Tools:
- palette knife
- piping bags
- cake cloth
- parchment paper strips, 1cm (0.4in) width, 18cm (7in) long

Cake:
- Square cake 15.25cm (6in), 15.25cm (6in) high

Buttercream:
- 600 gms (21oz) plain for crumb coating and final cover
- 100gms (3.5oz) light pink
- 100gms (3.5oz) light orange
- 100gms (3.5oz) light green
- 100gms (3.5oz) light yellow

GEOMETRIC TILES | 34

1. Mark the parchment paper strips with numbers (or letters) at the tip. This will help you identify which strip to pull first at the final step.

2. Directly after fully covering the surface of the cake with buttercream and smoothing it out, affix the parchment paper according to your desired design. Apply them in numbered order starting at one. If you wait too long, the frosting will dry, and the paper will not stick. If the surface has crusted already, you can apply a thin layer of vegetable shortening on to the strip so it can adhere better to the cake.

3. Use a piping bag to fill in the spaces between the parchment strips with your chosen colour of frosting. You can do this with solid colours for each space, multiple colours for a marbled effect, or even basic designs.

4. Use the flat edge of your palette knife to blend the frosting in the spaces between the parchment paper strips. Create a flat or lightly textured surface.

5. Wait until the buttercream surface has crusted before carefully removing the strips of parchment paper by pulling each one from the end. You must remove them in descending numerical/alphabetical order. This is because they overlap when you apply them in the beginning, and you do not want to pull them off all at the same time accidentally. Do this slowly to prevent any damage to the edges of the buttercream frosting.

6. Use the side of the palette knife or a toothpick to slightly flatten and smoothen the edges.

PRO TIP:

Prepare the parchment paper strips ahead of time. Number them at the tip so that you know the correct order to remove them at the end.

If you use a non-crusting type of frosting, chill the cake between steps three and five to make removal of the parchment strips easier.

Marvellous Mountains

Transform a delicious cake into a textured masterpiece with this unique sculptural decorating technique. Using masking technique, you can create landscapes, accents, and other designs. The process is simple, yet the results are nothing short of breathtaking.

You will need

Tools:
- palette knife
- piping bags
- cake cloth
- parchment paper

Cake:
- Top tier: Round cake, 10cm (4in) X 10cm (4in) high
- Bottom Tier: Round cake, 15cm (6in) X 15cm (6in) high

Buttercream:
- 1kg (35.2oz) plain for crumb coating and final cover
- 80 gms (2.8oz) grey
- 80 gms (2.8oz) light yellow
- 80 gms (2.8oz) golden yellow
- 80 gms (2.8oz) light pink
- 80 gms (2.8oz) white
- 80 gms (2.8oz) light green
- 80 gms (2.8oz) green
- 100gms (3.5oz) blue
- 100gms (3.5oz) Navy blue

1. Cover the surface of each cake tier with a gradient colour blend suitable for the project's final result. The image example uses green and yellow for a nature-inspired base (bottom-tier) and pink, golden yellow, yellow, and blue for a sunset sky overhead (top-tier). Leave small gaps between each colour for blending purposes.

2. Use the tip of your palette knife to spread each of the colours evenly to blend them together. Use short upward strokes to get the desired texture.

3. Tear a long piece of parchment paper into mountain or landscape shapes. You can also use your own design ideas to create a unique look. Carefully wrap this around each cake tier where you want the design to sit.

4. Use light blue, white, and a hint of dark blue to apply the mountain range design in the space between the parchment paper forms. Use your palette knife to make short upward and downward strokes to create a well-shaded effect.

5. Carefully peel the parchment paper away from the slightly crusted buttercream frosting. If you create a multi-layer design, wait a bit between each one to get a clean frosting edge.

6. Repeat this process for each cake tier or design layer.

Keep in mind that as objects move further away from the viewer, they tend to appear cooler (bluer), darker and less saturated. This is because the atmosphere scatters and absorbs light, making distant objects appear fainter and adopting the color of the sky (which is typically blue).

Remember this important technique to create the illusion of depth and distance in a two-dimensional artwork.

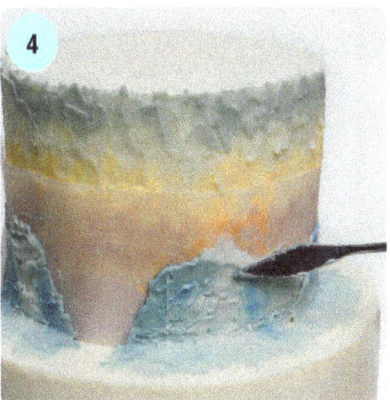

PRO TIP:

Use different colour combinations on the flat surface of the cake and for the landscape masked designs. This offers more decorative options especially for multi-tier cakes.

Gold Leaf Marble

This easy decorating idea suits any frosting colour combinations. It is a simple and quick way to make an impressive looking cake for any occasion. This style emphasizes expression of ideas, emotions, or concepts rather than the accurate representation of objects or scenes. Start with a selection of colours on a board for easy loading of your palette knife.

You will need

Tools:
- palette knife
- piping bags
- cake cloth
- edible gold leaf

Cake:
- Top tier: Round cake, 15cm (6in) X 10cm (4in) high
- Bottom Tier: Round cake, 20cm (8in) X 10cm (4in) high

Buttercream:
- 1kg (35.2oz) plain for crumb coating and final cover
- 80 gms (2.8oz) light green
- 80 gms (2.8oz) green
- 80 gms (2.8oz) blue
- 80 gms (2.8oz) dark brown
- 80 gms (2.8oz) white

1. After covering the cake with a neat layer of buttercream, choose the colours you want for this random blended design and space them out on a palette for easy use.

2. Load a short, angled palette knife with two or more colours at the same time for this unique blended effect. Then, simply apply them to the frosted cake in any direction you prefer.

3. You can go from the top toward the bottom, start in the middle, or make more abstract art in a random pattern.

4. Repeat on each tier. Be careful not to over-blend the colours.

5. Using tweezers, add strips or crumpled bits of edible gold leaf to the design you already created with the frosting. You can also use metallic paint as an alternative.

PRO TIP:

Choose your colour palette carefully to ensure a great-looking finished product.

When applying the frosting, be sure not to blend the colours together by pressing too hard or repeatedly blending with the palette knife. You want each to be visible in the design.

Pretty Patches

Create a stunning geometric cake with a unique colour palette of your choice. This simple yet impressive decorating idea can be applied to any shaped cakes. All you need are some varying sizes of palette knives and multiple colours of buttercream frosting to get this gorgeous effect.

You will need

Tools:
 - palette knife
- piping bags

Cake:
- Square cake 15.25cm (6in), 20cm (8in) high

Buttercream:
- 800 gms (28oz) plain for crumb coating and final cover
- 100gms (3.5oz) light grey
- 100gms (3.5oz) dark grey
- 100gms (3.5oz) light violet
- 100gms (3.5oz) dark violet
- 100gms (3.5oz) white

1. Use a short, angled palette knife to spread the different colours of frosting over the cake surface in overlapping strokes, rectangles, or random shapes. Start each stroke at the bottom and move your palette knife upward to get the pictured effect. (1A and 1B)

2. Choose a variety of wide-shaped palette knives next. Carefully go over the applied frosting to smooth any unattractive edges or to differentiate seams where things might have blended together too much. This also helps fill in any gaps between your colours. (2A and 2B)

3. Examine the whole surface of your decorated cake carefully to ensure even distribution of the different colours. Also look for gaps or thin spots that could use a bit more frosting.

PRO TIP:

Take care not to blend the colours together at the edges to prevent a muddy-looking result.

Clean your palette knife between each colour to prevent unattractive blending.

If you do not have a wide palette knife, simply cut a piece of sturdy plastic sheet into the desired shape.

PRETTY PATCHES | 41

Scenic Landscape

Design your own landscape scene by applying this easy palette knife painting blending technique. You may change the look by using a different colour moods or by moving around the different elements used in this project. Think of countryside settings such as fields, farms, rolling hills, and meadows and capture the beauty and the tranquility of nature.

You will need

Tools:
- palette knife
- piping bags

Cake:
- Round cake, 10cm (4in) X 7.5cm (3in) high
- Middle tier: Round cake, 15cm (6in) X 10cm (4in) high
- Bottom Tier: Round cake, 20cm (8in) X 7.5cm (3in) high

Buttercream:
- 1.2kg (42oz) plain for crumb coating and final cover
- 80 gms (2.8oz) light blue
- 80 gms (2.8oz) dark blue
- 80 gms (2.8oz) light yellow
- 80 gms (2.8oz) golden yellow
- 80 gms (2.8oz) brown
- 80 gms (2.8oz) plain buttercream
- 80 gms (2.8oz) golden yellow
- 80 gms (2.8oz) light green
- 80 gms (2.8oz) green
- 100gms (3.5oz) light violet
- 100gms (3.5oz) dark violet

1. Layer colours on the top tier to create a sunrise or sunset look. Use your palette knife to spread colours like blue, golden yellow, yellow, or pale below using a short or long upward stroke for each. You can be more playful and try circular or wavy strokes too.

2. Draw the outline for your landscape design using a toothpick or similar tool. This will help you visualize the final result before you begin applying frosting.

3. Prepare your chosen tinted buttercream palette in a board for ease of application. Each element can have a blended colour effect.

4. Either apply your frosting colours in the drawn designs and add the textures or load your palette knife with buttercream and individually add short random stroke designs to create a more natural flow for the landscape.

5. Repeat this until the entire artwork is complete. Add darker colours for shadows and lighter highlights for a more three-dimensional scene.

6. The bottom tier mimics a lavender field. Start by adding partitions using different shades of green and yellow tinted buttercream with very short strokes, almost just like a tapping motion to create small dots.

7. Complete the bottom tier with natural colours that you would find in the foreground of the beautiful lavender landscape. Finish off by creating tapping rows of purple and blue.

SCENIC LANDSCAPE | 43

Sunrise Over The Ocean

Create a glorious cake that shows off the true splendour of nature. Seascapes depict scenes along the coast, including beaches, cliffs, and oceans. You can capture the ever-changing moods of the sea, from calm and serene to stormy and dramatic. In just a few steps using your palette knife, you can create an amazing cake that will amaze and delight.

You will need

Tools:
- palette knife
- piping bags

Cake:
- Top tier: Round cake, 15cm (6in) X 15cm (6in) high
- Bottom Tier: Round cake, 20cm (8in) X 7.5cm (3in) high

Buttercream:
- 1kg (35.2oz) plain for crumb coating and final cover
- 100gms (3.5oz) light yellow
- 80 gms (2.8oz) yellow orange
- 80 gms (2.8oz) dark orange
- 80 gms (2.8oz) dark red
- 80 gms (2.8oz) dark Blue
- 80 gms (2.8oz) turquoise
- 120 gms (4.2oz) light blue
- 120 gms (4.2oz) medium shade blue
- 120 gms (4.2oz) light brown
- 80 gms (2.8oz) dark brown
- 80 gms (2.8oz) dark chestnut

1. Start on the top tier of the cake with the sunrise background design. Pipe appropriate colours around the entire cake and then even them out with your palette knife to create a nice blend. This gives an ombre effect that mimics the natural range of a sunrise.

2. Draw the sun location and any clouds with a toothpick. You can also freehand the clouds with blue and white frosting.

3. Follow the shape of the half circle with yellow and yellow orange frosting to create the sun's glow.

4. Continue the lower part of the top tier with dark blue colours that mimic ocean water. Use the palette knife horizontally in a gentle up and down motion to create the waves. Take care to make these look as smooth as possible so there are no unnatural seams going around the cake.

5. Draw the edge of the beach and the water with a toothpick. Fill in the associated places with the correct base colour of frosting first. Both of these blocks of colours will have a gradient from darker to lighter depending on your tastes.

6. Use white buttercream frosting on your palette knife to gently apply the crashing wave effect or sea spray to add a touch of realism. These should be short bouncing strokes that do not push the frosting into the background colour.

7. Using the same sunlight colours, load a new palette knife and gently tap or stroke the flow of light over the ocean waves.

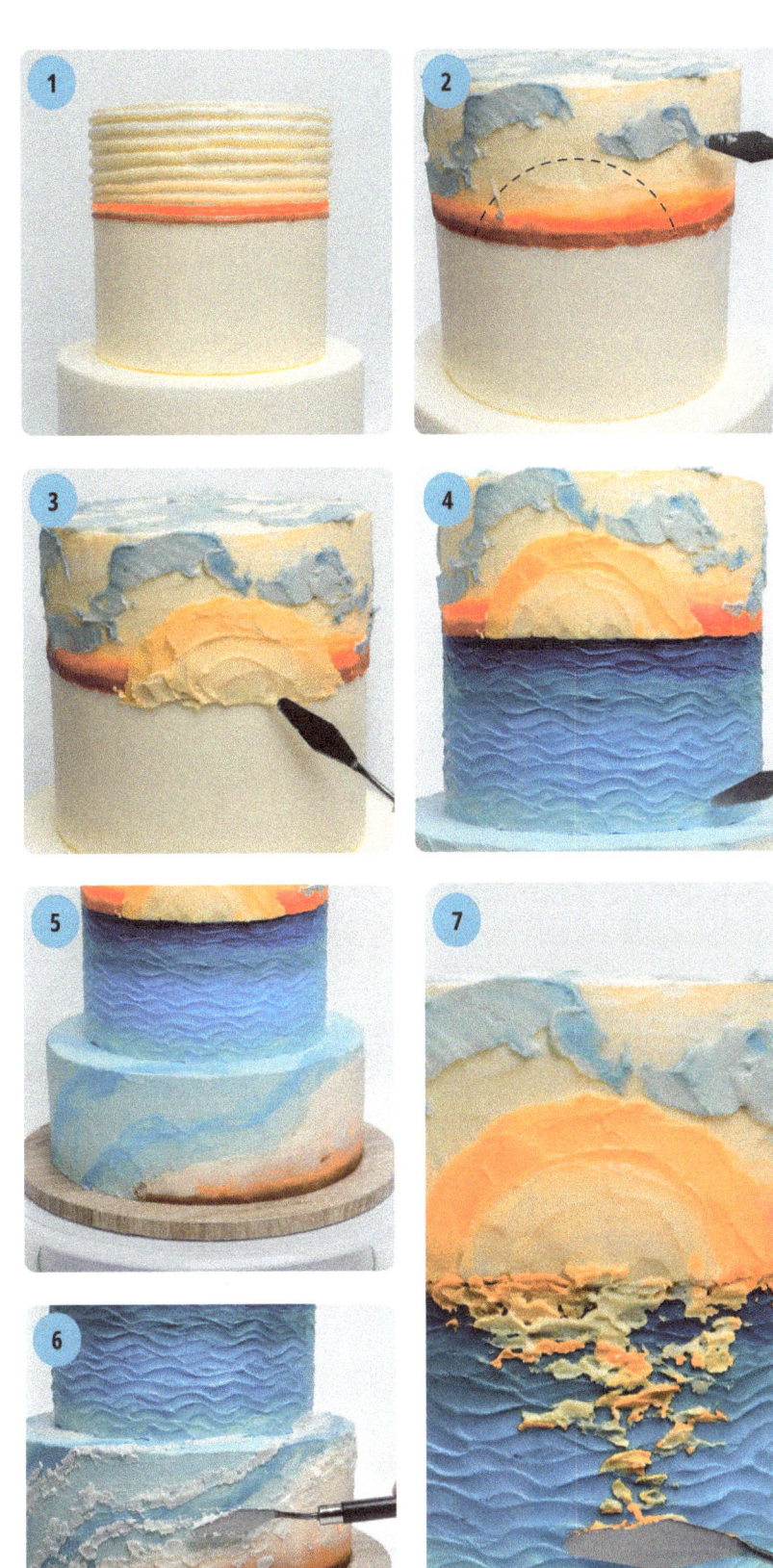

SUNRISE OVER THE OCEAN | 45

Fun Floral Dots

This simple yet impressive cake decorating design combines multi-hued dots with bold swirling flower accents. You can make a beautiful cake for any occasion in less time than you think. All it takes is a few frosting colours, a palette knife, and your imagination.

You will need

Tools:
- palette knife
- piping bags

Cake:
- Square cake 20cm (8in), 15.25cm (6in) high

Buttercream:
- 800 gms (28oz) plain for crumb coating and final cover
- 100gms (3.5oz) light green
- 100gms (3.5oz) green
- 100gms (3.5oz) light pink
- 100gms (3.5oz) pink with a hint of brown
- 150gms (5.3oz) light Aqua
- 150gms (5.3oz) light Aqua with a hint of brown
- 150gms (5.3oz) medium shade aqua

FUN FLORAL DOTS | 46

1. After you apply a smooth layer of buttercream frosting to the entire surface of the cake, use a toothpick to draw on the location of the final floral designs. This will help you complete the palette knife technique more easily.

2. Use a rounded-tip palette knife in your chosen size for the look you want at the end. Only load the blended buttercream colour onto the tip as you go. Angle it toward the circles that will end up being the flowers at the end. Gently press the frosting onto the cake and pull a short dot or petal design to create each element.

3. Continue this process overlapping each dot until the entire background from the edges of the cake to the circles is full. Change the colours slightly as you go for a unique, natural look. If you want to add the illusion of leaves, use a different green shade in that area of the cake surface.

4. Create the flower with a contrasting colour of frosting added in a circular motion to imitate ranunculus petals. Add a bit of texture with the tip of the palette knife.

5. Finally, add a green center accent to make the design look more like a flower and not just a circle.

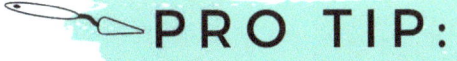

PRO TIP:

Change the shape of the circular flower if desired using your own artistic drawing ability or a cookie-cutter to outline the design.

Start with the outer edge of each cake side and work your way in toward the flower motif to get the desired effect.

FUN FLORAL DOTS | 47

Exquisite Tiles

This subtle yet beautiful cake decorating design that brings to mind gorgeous watercolour designs. Experiment with different colour palettes and follow these steps carefully to make an impressive display for your next cake project.

You will need

Tools:
- palette knife
- piping bags
- bendy scraper

Cake:
- Round cake, 20cm (8in) X 20cm (8in) high

Buttercream:
- 800 gms (28oz) plain for crumb coating and final cover
- 100gms (3.5oz) white
- 100gms (3.5oz) light blue
- 100gms (3.5oz) dark blue
- 100gms (3.5oz) dark brown
- 100gms (3.5oz) dark aqua

1. Prepare all your colours on a board before you start decorating the cake. Combine different shades of tinted buttercream and load it on the tip of the palette knife or the thick plastic sheet to make a marbled or watercolour effect on the final design.

2. Start at the bottom of the cake and work around the circumference. Load the palette knife (or thick plastic sheet) with the first colour and create a short, relatively square tile using an alternating upward and sideward stroke. Keep the knife parallel to the surface of the cake as much as possible for smooth application.

3. Repeat the same steps moving around the cake in alternating upward and sideward strokes. You can use various gradient colours to create a stunning marble effect per tile.

4. Complete the top of the cake with spiral or concentric circles using the same palette knife technique.

 **PRO TIP:**

Use a cut plastic sheet as a tool if you do not have a wide palette knife in your cake decorating toolbox.

Repeat each circle if tiles around the cake completely before adding the next. Overlap the frosting application slightly while taking care not to blend the colours together.

EXQUISITE TILES | 49

Stunning Spades

This stunning repeating pattern technique using your pointed tip palette knife offers a limitless look on your cake design. How you will build up the shading of every colour and the direction of every stroke will determine the final look of your cake. With this project, you may create your own masterpiece design a lot quicker that you expect.

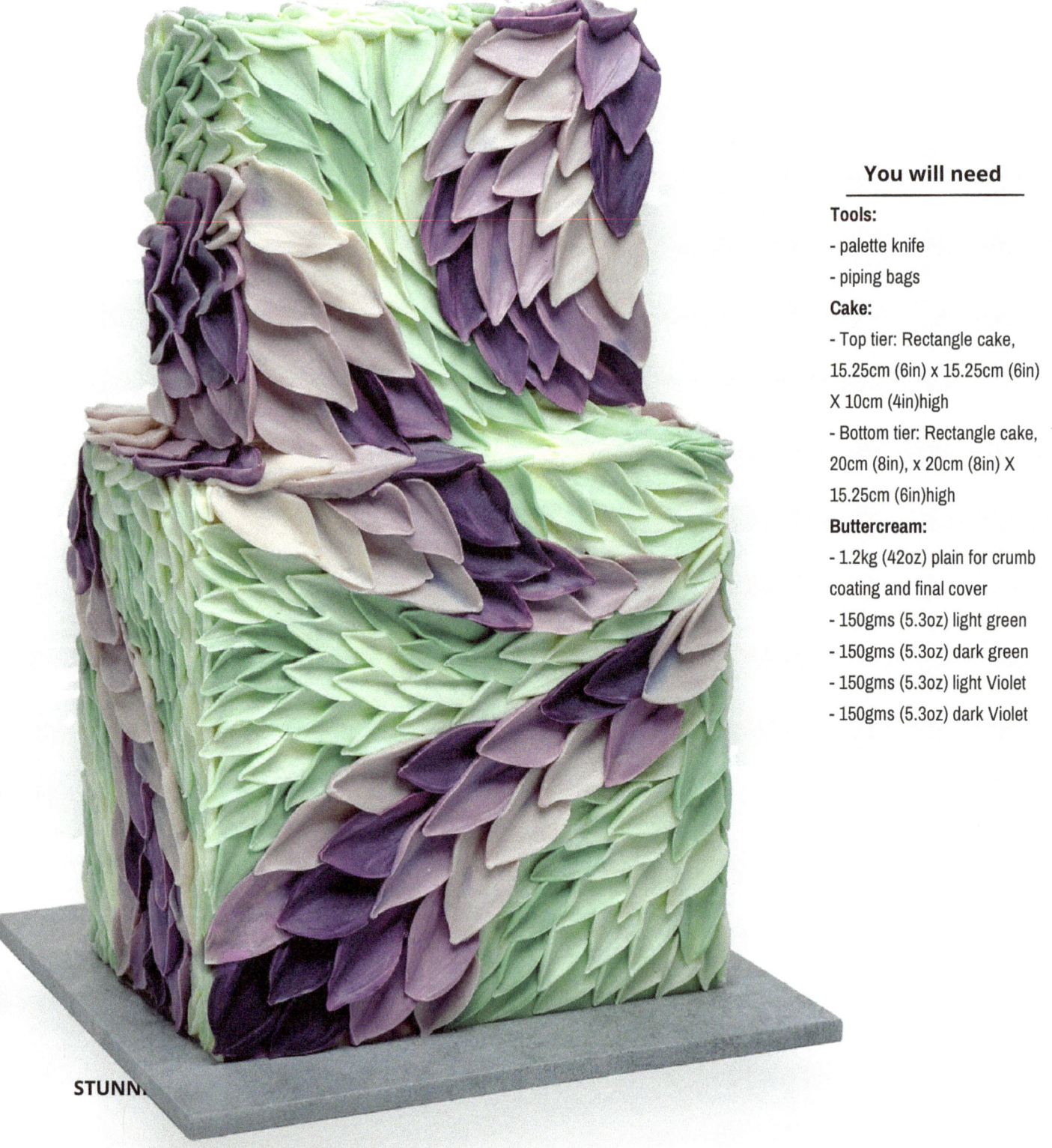

You will need

Tools:
- palette knife
- piping bags

Cake:
- Top tier: Rectangle cake, 15.25cm (6in) x 15.25cm (6in) X 10cm (4in)high
- Bottom tier: Rectangle cake, 20cm (8in), x 20cm (8in) X 15.25cm (6in)high

Buttercream:
- 1.2kg (42oz) plain for crumb coating and final cover
- 150gms (5.3oz) light green
- 150gms (5.3oz) dark green
- 150gms (5.3oz) light Violet
- 150gms (5.3oz) dark Violet

1. Start with spreading a thin layer or line of a guide colour onto the spaces of the cake where you intend to make the repeating pattern. You can also draw lines or shapes with a toothpick if that suits your decorating needs better.

2. Gently blend to green colours together for the first repeating pattern areas if you want the same design as shown in these pictures. Each detail is made by loading a moderate amount of buttercream on the back of the palette knife, gently pressing it onto the prepared cake, and pulling away slowly to create the grooved shape. Use this same process over and over again to overlap the details and fill in the areas.

3. Repeat the same process until you fill the spaces with your chosen colours and size of details.

4. Use your alternative colour blend to fill in the other spaces that match the guide colours or the drawn shapes on the cake surface. This is done with a larger palette knife to create differentiation between the green and purple sections. Follow the natural contours of the lines you chose as you see in the pictures.

 PRO TIP:

Try a different look by alternating the direction of the palette knife movement from one coloured section to the next. Press and pull the buttercream frosting in the opposite way.

Make sure there are no gaps between the details or sections of colour.

Groovy Shells

This truly unique palette knife decorating idea works on any shape cake. It is ideal for dramatic displays as seen in the pictures with a variety of colours. You can also try a more monochromatic effect and let the texture do the work for style.

You will need

Tools:

- palette knife
- piping bags

Cake:

- Round cake, 20cm (8in) X 7.5cm (3in) high

Buttercream:

- 400gms (14oz) plain for crumb coating and final cover
- 150gms (5.3oz) light caramel
- 150gms (5.3oz) light caramel
- 150gms (5.3oz) light grey
- 150gms (5.3oz) salmon

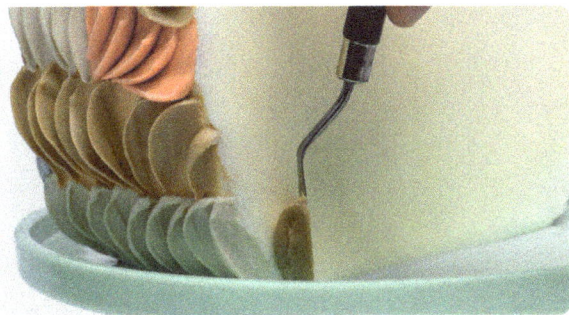

1. Use a short-angled palette knife with a large amount of buttercream frosting on the back side. Hold the edge of the knife against the cake surface with the blade approximately 45 degrees out. We suggest starting at the bottom part of the cake. Use the side stroke technique to create each element.

2. Press the frosting in a thick ridged layer and then sweep the palette knife tighter to the surface of the cake to affix it. This makes the blade of the knife become parallel or flat on the surface of the cake as you move it. Repeat this process to create a layered shell effect as seen in the image. Each repeating pattern should cover a gentle arc shape that points a varying direction than the others around it.

3. Alternate colours in your chosen palette so that no two adjacent groovy shells are the same. Adapt the direction of the shells to the space you are trying to fill. In this image, the strokes are now upward.

4. Especially for this shape of a cake, it is best to start on the bottom or edge and work your way continuously around without leaving any gaps.

5. Continue the same multi-layered sweeps until the entire surface of the cake is covered. Ensure that the edges are covered sufficiently with the different colours of frosting so there are no unattractive seams.

PRO TIP:

Create this "standing cake" or "top-forward cake" style by cutting about an inch off the bottom of the cake to make it stand on its side and resemble a semi-circle.

For cake edges and the bottom near the stand, pull the palette knife to the side instead of sweeping it downward.

Create a more refined pattern by keeping all the grooved shells facing the same direction. Also, try different sizes of coloured groovy shells for a variation and unique look.

GROOVY SHELLS | 53

Impressionist

Impressionist style of painting, often characterized by visible and loose strokes. Use short, varying thickness of strokes to create a sense of movement and spontaneity. The goal is to capture the essence of a scene quickly and directly.

Style Art

Impressionist paintings tend to have a lack of fine, intricate details when viewed up close. The focus was on the overall effect and the interplay of colors, rather than on precisely rendering every aspect of a scene. This style embraces a more personal and subjective interpretation of reality, often using unconventional angles and viewpoints.

Freehand Fleurs

The soft textures and blended colours of impressionistic painting comes to your cake decorating repertoire with this lovely freehand design. Simple palette knife techniques can create any range of options for the perfect spring or summer design. Follow along for the white blossoms on a pink background or choose your own favourite shades for a unique look.

You will need

Tools:

- palette knife
- piping bags

Cake:

- Top tier: Round cake, 15cm (6in) X 15cm (6in)
- Bottom Tier: Round cake, 20cm (8in) X 10cm (4in) high

Buttercream:

- 400gms (14oz) plainfor crumb coating
- 500gms (14oz) light pink
- 100gms (3.5oz) dark pink
- 100gms (3.5oz) light pink
- 100gms (3.5oz) light green
- 100gms (3.5oz) dark green
- 150gms (5.3oz) White

FREEHAND FLEURS | 56

1. Focus on capturing the general outline and proportions of the leaves. Begin with multiple colours of green blended together and use short strokes to create the leaves that are at the background of every floral motif.

2. Use a medium amount of buttercream frosting on the back of the palette knife and curve it in a relatively circular motion to create each bud or petal in the background.

3. Create the main flower petals with white tinted buttercream using a larger palette knife with wider strokes. Join four or more petals together per flower and position the flowers in different angles throughout the cake. Add the center yellow or green dot to indicate the center of each large flower.

4. Finally, layer more leaves and a few smaller petals or buds to fill in gaps in your design. Do this in multiple steps to create a more natural garden look.

PRO TIP:

Before you start painting, prepare a range of colors you'll need for the flowers, leaves, and background. Since palette knife painting often involves bold strokes and layering, having a variety of colors mixed and ready is important.

Use colours to create the idea of a particular type of flower instead of trying to draw the precise shape.

As you progress, layer the buttercream using the palette knife. Apply thick strokes to create texture and dimension in the petals and leaves. You can use different angles of the palette knife to achieve various effects.

Shades of Fall

In this cake design comes alive with the vibrant and warm hues of the fall season. The scene is set in a tranquil countryside landscape, where nature is awash in the colours of autumn. It is filled with trees, their leaves transformed into a breathtaking tapestry of reds, oranges, and yellows. These trees create a natural archway overhead, their branches intermingling in a whimsical dance.

You will need

Tools:
- palette knife
- piping bags
- toothpick
- bendy scraper

Cake:
- Top tier: Round cake:
  15cm (6in) X 10cm (4in) high
- Bottom Tier: Round cake:
  20cm (8in) X 15cm (6in) high

Buttercream:
- 1kg (35.2oz) plain for crumb coating and final cover
- 100gms (3.5oz) white
- 100gms (3.5oz) blue
- 40gms (1.4oz) grey
- 80 gms (2.8oz) dark Blue
- 80 gms (2.8oz) light green
- 80 gms (2.8oz) dark green
- 100gms (3.5oz) dark brown
- 100gms (3.5oz) golden yellow
- 100gms (3.5oz) Caramel
- 80 gms (2.8oz) orange
- 80 gms (2.8oz) yellow
- 80 gms (2.8oz) red

1. Start by outlining the entire drawing design on the surface of the prepared cake. Use a toothpick to position the elements like a river, bridge, and beautiful autumn trees.

2. Fill one element at a time with the desired background colour. Use toothpicks to add detailed lines and grooves.

3. Create a lovely sky effect with lighter blue and white buttercream on the palette knife. Use gentle circular strokes for a soft dimensional effect.

4. Blend medium and lighter tones of blue for the water of the river. Create gentle textures like wave motion as this part of the artwork disappears under the bridge. Small white frosting taps with a palette knife look like reflected sunlight on the waves.

5. Cover the entire background of the cake with light caramel and golden yellow or similar coloured frosting to create a rough autumn backdrop for the trees and other foliage elements.

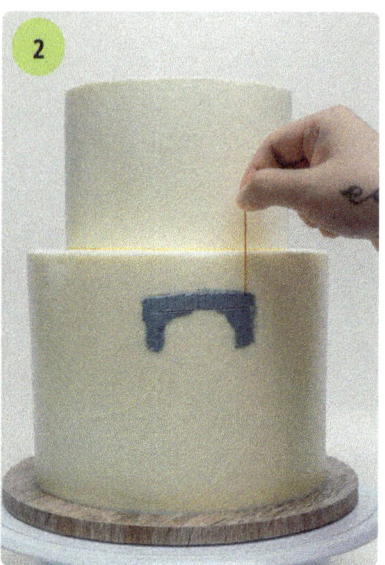

SHADES OF FALL | 60

6. Add some elements on the side of the river like bushes using short and tapping strokes. Create some greenery effect on the top part of the bottom tier using varying shades of green in small circular strokes. This will mimic the lush leaves of the distant rows of trees in the background.

7. Load the palette knife with multiple shades of dark or medium brown to draw in the trunks of the trees and branches stretching overhead into the top tier of the cake. Add lighter brown highlights as desired to mimic the wood grain or bark design.

8. Use the same tapping technique and overlap the colours starting with orange, then yellow and then brilliant reds, for the fall leaves covering the branches. Darker browns work well for shadows under the trees or the illusion of stones near the riverbank.

9. Use a fresh palette knife with green or golden colours to roughly tap in bushes and other plants around the river and the base of the trees. This would give the impression of fallen leaves. Add some more tree trunks to create more balance to the whole scenery.

Pay attention to perspective in your autumn art design. The closest tree trunks should be larger than those in the background.

Try these similar techniques for a lovely spring or summer time seeing with brighter greens or even the flowers in the trees.

SHADES OF FALL | 61

Fresh Fruit Basket

Create a beautiful fruit basket cake that is sweeter than the real thing. The unique palette knife technique used on the bottom tier creates a realistic weave design that complements well with the colourful fruits on top. Go playful and use the strokes in this project to create another look for your basket and other types of fruits.

You will need

Tools:
- palette knife
- piping bags

Cake:
- Top tier: Round cake 15cm (6in) X 10cm (4in)
- Bottom Tier: Round cake 20cm (8in) X 7.5m (3in) high

Buttercream:
- 400gms (14oz) plain for crumb coating
- 400gms (14oz) light grey for final cover
- 150gms (5.3oz) Brown with a hint of red
- 100gms (3.5oz) dark brown
- 100gms (3.5oz) red
- 80 gms (2.8oz) white
- 80 gms (2.8oz) light yellow
- 80 gms (2.8oz) light caramel with a hint of brown
- 80 gms (2.8oz) light violet
- 80 gms (2.8oz) dark violet
- 80 gms (2.8oz) light green
- 80 gms (2.8oz) dark green

FRESH FRUIT BASKET | 63

1. Cover the larger bottom tier of a two-tier cake with dark brown frosting, add an extra amount of frosting about an inch on the top edge to create a basket like shape. The top tier is covered with light grey to make a pleasant fruit background. Then, use a wide plastic scraper to create vertical lines around the basket for the woven section design.

2. Use the tip of a palette knife to create the woven texture. Each one is a downward curving stroke between the vertical lines you made in step one. Continue to surround the entire base of the cake.

3. Use white and light brown tinted buttercream and go over some of the weaves to create some highlight and use dark brown for the shadow effect. Add as much shadowing colours as you like similar to main project photo.

4. With a clean toothpick or similar tool, draw the outline of grapes, apples, lemons, or other fruit on the top tier. As you see in the pictures, also draw the grapes or other elements cascading over the basket on the bottom.

5. Start with the outermost details in the whole picture. With the back of the palette knife, use gently blended colours of green for the leaves.

FRESH FRUIT BASKET

6. Start with the furthest away elements on the fruit basket level. In this case, we began with the pear and then the grapes with their appropriate colours.

7. Details to the grapes were added using a darker violet tinted buttercream and small circular motion. Use light or dark frosting as a final layer in certain spots.

8. Add the rest of the fruits. As you work through the different types of fruit, remember the idea of shadows and highlights to make them look more dimensional.

9. Paint smaller details such as stems, leaves, and any unique features of the fruit.

10. For fruit designs on top of the basket weave frosting, use a piping bag to first lay down the base colour before decorating with the palette knife. You can also flatten those sections of the woven texture with a clean knife before adding the fruit design. Add small strawberry seeds with a toothpick and a tiny amount of frosting or with a piping bag with a very tiny hole at the tip.

Gradually layer colors to achieve depth and dimension. Blend colors where necessary to achieve a smooth transition between shades.

Use different strokes and palette knife techniques to replicate the textures of the fruit's skin. This might involve dabbing, stippling, or using short, directional strokes.

FRESH FRUIT BASKET | 65

Mysterious Maiden

Translate your favourite subject to an artistic design on your cake using simple palette knife strokes. Embrace the spontaneity and freedom of this style to create a unique and expressive portrait. This project is visually satisfying as you observe the movement of every stroke and the importance of every shade of colour..

You will need

Tools:
- palette knife
- piping bags
- cake cloth
- parchment paper

Cake:
Round cake:
20cm (8in) X 20cm (8in) high

Buttercream:
- 800 gms (28oz) plain for crumb coating and final cover
- 100gms (3.5oz) brown
- 100gms (3.5oz) chestnut
- 100gms (3.5oz) pink
- 100gms (3.5oz) caramel
- 150gms (5.3oz) black
- 60gms (2.1oz) violet
- 60gms (2.1oz) red
- 80 gms (2.8oz) green

1. Cover the whole surface of the cake with slightly overlapping tiles of multi-hued or solid colour buttercream frosting (see Exquisite Tiles). Trace a silhouette of a side portrait view on a piece of parchment paper using buttercream in a seamless piping bag with a small hole at the tip. Then, carefully press this onto the surface of the cake so that the frosting transfers to the solid surface. (see Templates) Focus on getting the placement of eyes, nose, mouth, and ears right.

2. Use a palette knife or cake cloth to flatten the buttercream inside the outline of the portrait pattern. Then, fill in and even out the face part with a light caramel tinted buttercream using a short angled palette knife to establish the basic values (lightness and darkness) of the portrait.

3. Begin layering colors gradually, building up the form of the face. Create the illusion of shadows and contouring with slightly darker shades or other delicate colours. Applying colorful buttercream is optional. You can also opt for skintone shades instead.

4. You can use a cocktail stick or toothpick to outline the facial details and then apply the closed eye lashes and brow with black and the lips with pink or red tinted buttercream. You can use a small pointy palette knife or a piping bag with a very small hole at the tip to do this.

5. Repeat the same process and add a darker shade to create a blended shadow along the neck, jaw line, and back.

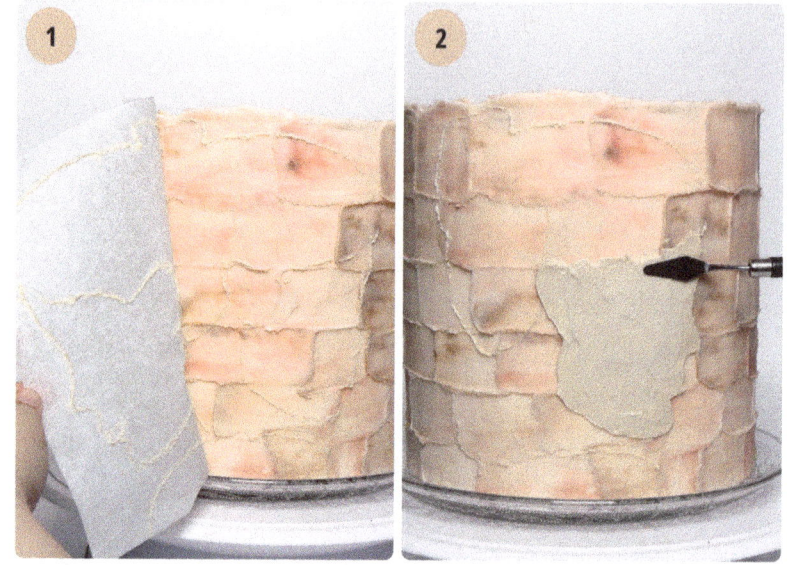
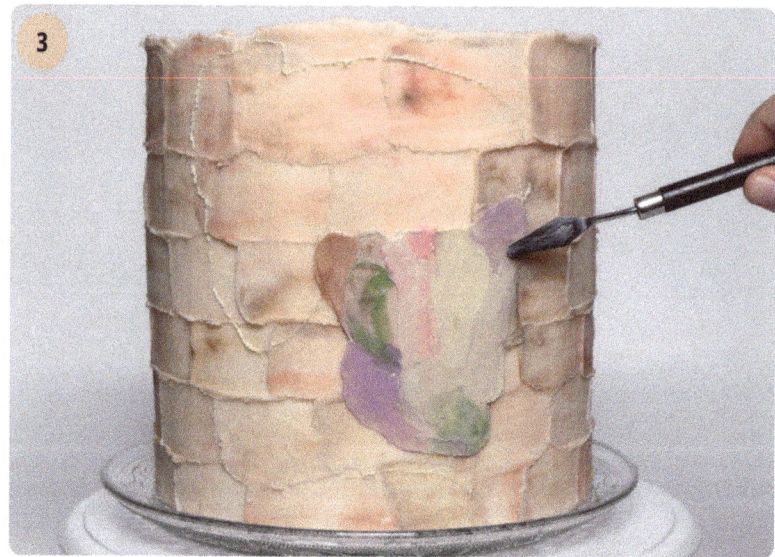

MYSTERIOUS MAIDEN | 68

6. Move on to painting the hair. Hair can be challenging due to its texture and complexity, so observe the direction of hair strands and use varying strokes. Fill in the hair with black tinted buttercream or another desired colour using a small circular motion with the tip of the knife. You can leave a space for light coloured floral details to avoid colour-through of the black tinted buttercream.

7. To give a highlight, use white tinted buttercream and repeat the circular motion on some parts of the hair.

8. Create a coloured floral design on the hair with your choice of colours. Start with green leaves in the background and then blue and purple spots to indicate petals of the lovely blossoms. Use either press and slide or press and curve strokes to do the blossoms.

9. Fill the rest of the space with light blue petals and more leaves to add variation. Repeat the same steps and add floral design on the bottom part of the cake.

Eyes, nose, and mouth are crucial parts of the portrait. Observe the shapes and colors carefully.

Work from larger areas to smaller details. Pay attention to subtle color shifts on the skin due to lighting and shadows. Blend edges between colors to avoid harsh lines.

Creating an impressionist portrait involves using loose spontaneous strokes, playful colors, and an emphasis on capturing the mood and essence of the subject rather than focusing on precise details.

MYSTERIOUS MAIDEN | 69

Scarlet the Parrot

.This design is a captivating fusion of color, light, and emotion that transports you into a world where the beauty of nature is captured through simple palette knife strokes. It offers a fresh and evocative interpretation of a bird's existence in its natural habitat, leaving a lasting impression. Design a cake with your favourite animal or pet by using nothing else but your small palette knife and colourful frosting.

You will need

Tools:
- palette knife
- piping bags
- parchment paper

Cake:
- Top tier: Square cake: 10cm (4in), 7.5Cm (3in) high
- Bottom tier: Square cake: 15.25cm (6in), 20cm (8in) high

Buttercream:
- 800 gms (28oz) light brown
- 80 gms (2.8oz) light brown
- 80 gms (2.8oz) dark brown
- 80 gms (2.8oz) dark green
- 80 gms (2.8oz) light green
- 80 gms (2.8oz) red
- 60gms (2.1oz) yellow
- 60gms (2.1oz) pink
- 60gms (2.1oz) orange
- 60gms (2.1oz) white
- 60gms (2.1oz) black
- 60gms (2.1oz) violet
- 80 gms (2.8oz) light blue
- 80 gms (2.8oz) dark Blue

SCARLET THE PARROT | 71

1. Cover the entire surface of the cake with a slightly marbled buttercream finish (see Marbling technique). Use the pattern transfer technique to get the shape of the parrot to the surface of the cake. Use a piping bag to apply an outline to the pattern and all necessary details. (see Mysterious Maiden and Templates)

2. Use the palette knife loaded with multiple green shades to tap or dab on textured background to mimic leaves. Also add touches of red or blue (or other colours) to indicate flowers or fruit growing in that habitat. Do not cover the space for the bird.

3. Start with the base colors of the parrot. Identify the main colors on the parrot's body and wings. Start with the background colour, which is red in the case of this parrot and use short or long strokes as appropriate.

4. Begin adding details and layers to your parrot. Work from the background to the foreground, gradually adding more intricate details. Start with broader strokes and gradually refine the details as you go along. Repeat the same process until all the details are done. Be careful not to blend the colours as you go as you want each stroke to mimic the lovely feathers.

5. Fill the face with white and black tinted buttercream for the beak. Use a small and pointy palette knife for this. Alternatively, you can use a seamless piping bag with a small hole at the tip to carefully fill in the details.

6. Focus on the parrot's eyes and beak. These are important features that can bring your painting to life. Use a toothpick or the piping bag to add the fine details on the eyes and face.

7. For the tree branch, fill it with medium brown tinted buttercream and spread it evenly with a short rounded palette knife. You can us a piping bag or apply the brown tinted buttercream directly with a palette knife. Leave it with some uneven lines to create lovely wood textures.

8. Finally, with a very light touch of white, dark brown, or black tinted, apply it on the tree branch to give highlights and accents.

9. Use black tinted buttercream for the claws.

Take your time to capture the unique textures of the feathers. Observe how the feathers overlap and create depth. Use a variety of strokes to mimic the different types of feathers.

Add shadows and highlights to your painting to create dimension. Identify the light source in your reference image and apply shadows where appropriate. Use lighter shades to highlight the areas where light hits the parrot or your subject.

SCARLET THE PARROT | 73

2 Dimensional

Creating a floral painting with two dimensional palette knife painting technique can result in vibrant and expressive artworks. Mix various shades and tones to capture the depth and vibrancy of the flowers.

Techniques

Use different angles and pressures to create varied textures and thicknesses of buttercream. The palette knife can be used to create bold strokes, intricate details, and layered effects. This technique allows you to create slightly raised textures on the canvas.

Leaves & Ferns

Foliage can perform several functions in a design. You can use leaves to really set up or frame a flower, or to fill spaces between design elements. Adding leaves can bring depth, texture, and a sense of realism to your artwork. observe your reference image or real leaves to determine the colors needed. Mix various shades of green, as well as other colors like yellow, red, and brown for more realistic variation. Below are some examples of different shapes of foliage and ferns. Use different palette knives in varying shapes to achieve the overall look. You can use a piping bag with a very small tip or toothpick/cocktail stick to add the veins or fine details.

Fillers & Wild Flowers

Filler flowers are often smaller, delicate blooms that are used to complement and enhance the main flowers in floral arrangements. They help add texture, volume, and a sense of fullness to bouquets and centerpieces. Filler flowers can also provide a touch of color and can be used to create a harmonious transition between different types of flowers. Here are some examples of common filler flowers:

FILLERS & WILDFLOWERS | 77

Lavender

Introduce the lovely look of lavender in your next cake decorating project. Lavender flowers are typically small, clustered in elongated spikes. They come in various shades of purple, from pale lavender to deep violet.

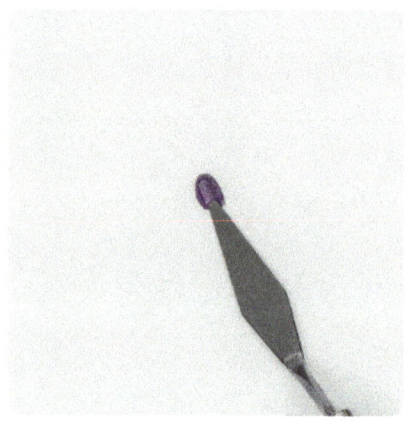

1. Use the smallest and pointy palette knife in your toolbox. Loaded with a very small amount of purple blended buttercream, dab it onto the surface, press and pull away gently to create a small bud.

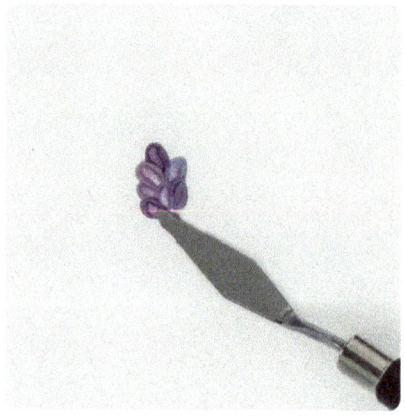

2. Repeat this process on both sides of the centerline for the lavender profiler stalk. Be sure to overlap the individual buds to give it a full, natural look.

3. Continue with the same steps until you get the desired length per stalk.

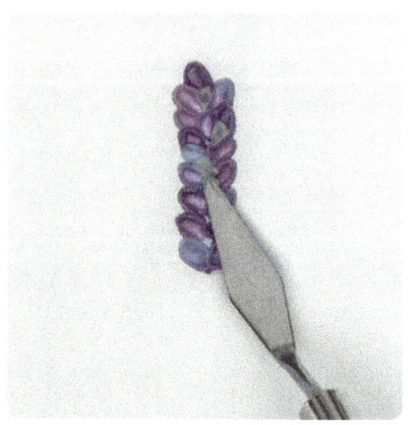

4. Add white or a paler accent colour with the same palette knife technique for highlights.

5. Then, finish up the lavender blossom with caramel frosting to make the flower design look more realistic.

PRO TIP:

Make a cluster of the palette knife painted dots to give the illusion of a lovely lavender bouquet. You do not have to create every individual bud that would be on a real flower.

Jasmine

Jasmine flowers are typically white or cream-colored, but some varieties are yellow or pink blossoms. They are often small, trumpet-shaped, and have five or more petals. These simple press and slide flowers are easy to make for beginners but make a beautiful impact on any cake.

1. Use a rounded tip palette knife and use press and slide stroke to create a natural petal shape. Use a plain or white tinted buttercream. A single petal can represent a delicate bud. (see Basic Strokes)

2. Use a seamless piping bag with a tiny hole at the tip to pipe the stem.

3. For variation, you can combine two petals for a different look.

4. Combine layers of petals for a side facing flower. Make sure to add a dot in the center.

5. Create a full jasmine flower with five surrounding a central point. Turn your palette knife as you work. Try different angles and sizes to give your final design more interest. Finish the design using a small piping bag of green for the stamen, caps, and stems and make sure to add a central dot in each blossom.

Hydrangea

These lovely and popular flowers make a big impact on a floral themed cake. These clusters of small flowers in bloom: blue, purple, pink, and white cluster together to create the impressive bunches that are popular in wedding bouquets and decorations.

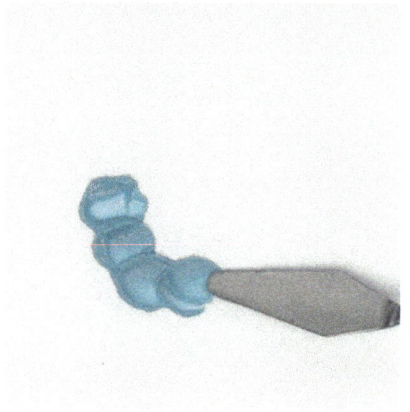

1. Start with darker blue tones either on the left or on the right side to create accents and shadows for your hydrangea flower. Each one is made with the rounded tip of your palette knife. Simply press the frosting gently on the surface and then pull away to create a small circular design. (see Basic Strokes)

2. Move toward pale blue and white petals as you finish shaping the flower.

3. Work around the exterior circle first and then fill in the center with additional small flower petals. Turn the palette knife as you go to keep the rounded tip of the palette knife and toward the outside of the hydrangea.

3. Keep lighting in mind when deciding where to put the lightest tones as you fill the center of the flower.

PRO TIP:

Remember that natural hydrangea flowers can include blue, pink, white, and other colours. Try your own special look.

Use a very small amount of buttercream frosting for each petal to avoid excess thickness that would hide the rounded shape.

Violet

Violets are pretty flowers that many people associate with youth and shyness. However, your cake does not need to take a backseat when you use this type of blossoms in the decorating style. They are simple and quick to make with your palette knife and pack a lot of impact with their rich colours.

1. Violets are another flower that uses the press and slide technique with a palette knife. Choose a dark or bright purple shade loaded on the tip of a rounded knife. Keep the handle pointed toward the center as you work around the five petals.

2. Use the press and slide technique to create the petals that all go towards the center. (see Basic Strokes)

PRO TIP:

Violets also come in different shades of purple, so you have many options for unique designs.

Create the leaves first if including them on your cake. Also make one or two small buds in each flower cluster.

3. Use a toothpick to finish each violet flower with small yellow or white dots in the center. Create single blossoms or clusters depending on the overall layout of your floral decorations.

Dogwood

Decorate a cake with some of the earliest signs of spring with the flowering dogwood tree design. The larger blossoms can come in white as shown and soft pink shades. The details are what make all the difference.

1. Use a round-tipped palette knife to create four small petals equally spaced from each other for the classic dogwood shape using press and slide stroke. Keep the handle of the knife pointed toward the center and do not press too hard as you pull the knife off the surface. (see Basic Strokes)

2. Use the tip of a rounded or pointed palette knife to remove a semicircular divot of white frosting from the center edge of each petal. Dogwood tree flowers have this unique edge design.

3. Create the textured center of the dogwood flower by gently pushing green buttercream frosting through a sieve or strainer.

4. Collect a small dab on the end of a toothpick and carefully position it where the petals meet in the middle.

5. Use a light brown tinted buttercream in a seamless piping bag to pipe a thin outline on the divots.

PRO TIP:

The flowering dogwood tree has bold dark green leaves. Create these before you put the flowers on top for a natural springtime look.

Freesia

Lovely freesia flowers are popular spring and summertime blossoms for bouquets and decorations of all kinds. Now you can create these bright and delicate designs on your next cake with a very simple palette knife technique.

1. Use a small, rounded tip palette knife to create the buds and five petals on each individual flower. This uses the same press and slide technique. For a side facing flower, start with a cluster of three petals joined together. (see Basic Strokes)

2. Add the center of the flower with a bright orange dot as well as the bottom layer of petals that are arranged wider than the outer layer.

3. Create the five petals for a full bloom look. Keep the handle of the palette knife pointed toward the center as you make each petal.

3. Finish the full blossoms with a dot in the center. Finally, use a soft spring green shade to create each flower cup and the curved stem they are all attached to, like in the main photo.

PRO TIP:

Freesias come in a variety of colours so try pinks, yellow, and white. Try other colours in your next project.

Each stock should have a succession of full blossoms, half-closed flowers, and buds.

Pansy

The happy faces of pansy flowers bring springtime to mind. With simple techniques and bright colours, you can easily create a collection of blossoms to suit any cake design.

1. Start with the two dark purple petals at the top of the pansy as these are farthest away and at the back of the flower. Use a rounded-tip palette knife to create an almost circular shape with a thin ridge at the outer edge. Use either press and slide or press and curve strokes to achieve this petal shape. (see Basic Strokes)

2. Continue with the two lighter purple petals that overlap the dark ones at least halfway. These are essentially parallel to each other with the new petals slightly larger than the darker ones in the background.

3. Angle the palette knife so the tip is pointing downward at an angle to create the yellow petals next. These are the same size as the pale purple ones you just completed.

4. Use a piping bag with a very small hole at the tip and black tinted buttercream to create the center stamens. This looks like a short array of lines spreading out over the inner portion of all petals.

Daisy

Bright happy daisies make for a beautiful cake decoration design. Go for classic white or any combination of yellow, orange, and pink if you want a more colourful painted daisy motif.

1. Use the press and slide technique of making elongated flower petals. For the daisy, these are longer than other flowers, so start with more frosting than for small, round petals. (see Basic Strokes)

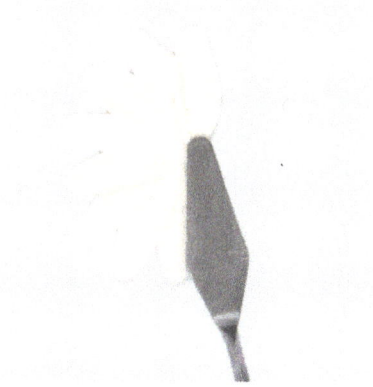

2. Repeat the same technique over and over until you create a circle of similar petals. Rotate your palette knife so the handle points toward the center of the flower.

3. Blend yellow and light orange frosting together and pass it through a small-hole strainer/sieve. Transfer the resulting accent to the center of the daisy flower using a toothpick. (see Dogwood)

4. Add an optional second layer of petals to create a unique daisy design. Another option is to create a flat daisy from a side view.

5. After finishing an array of petals, add the center yellow accent at the top join.

PRO TIP:

You can lightly sketch the outline of your daisies and any other elements in your composition with a piping bag using the same colour of the daisies. This will serve as a rough guide to make sure you will be able to keep the shape and placement of your flowers.

DAISY | 85

Anthurium

Exotic, tropical anthurium flowers make a stunning design for your next cake. These large and brilliantly coloured blooms are simple to make with your palette knife skills.

1. Use a very large pointy palette knife with a wide blade. Load it with a large amount of the main buttercream frosting colour.

2. Press the frosting firmly against the surface until the buttercream extends to the side of the palette knife creating a wide shape petal.

3. Drag the knife down to create the correct shape of the main flower petal. Move it slightly side to side if necessary for the spade-like shape. (see Basic Strokes)

4. Shape the base of the petal by cleaning off any excess buttercream with a clean palette knife.

5. Use a piping bag with yellow frosting to pipe a thick line down the center of the main red flower part. It should be wider at the base of the petal and narrow until about three-quarters the length of the petal.

6. Add a dotted texture to the center line with a toothpick or a piping bag with a small hole at the tip.

Poppy

The brilliant red colour of poppies brings a touch of style to any summertime cake. These techniques cover full-blown flowers with their prominent black centers and pretty buds for unique cake decorating looks.

1. Start by finishing the back petals of the poppy using a couple of side stroke petals. Angle the loaded knife at around 45 degrees before drawing it down to layer the frosting in the side-angle flower view. It can be three or more petals. (see Basic Strokes)

2. Use a small piping bag to pipe the black spikes and green tinted buttercream for the main center using a piping bag or the strainer/sieve technique. (see Dogwood)

3. Continue the rest of the poppy's closest petals. Make the left-side petal first (if you are right-handed) using a downward stroke toward the center.

4. Finally, finish the center with a broad, flat petal under the black and green center. Make sure the bottom line of the entire flower is solid and smooth. It can also be the same number of outer petals or more.

5. Create a flat-open poppy using the same angled palette knife technique all the way around the center spot. This view has four to six petals only.

6. Pipe black spikes with a piping bag and the green center accent in a circular design. (see Dogwood)

POPPY | 87

Camellia

The robust, multi-hued flowers of class camellias can decorate your next cake with beauty. This unique layered petal design gives unending options for full blossoms and buds.

1. Create the flower bud by loading the tip of the palette knife with your main colour frosting. Use the press and curve stroke gently and do not slide the tip of the knife very far. Instead, move it in a circular motion to create a round bud. (see Basic Strokes)

2. Repeat the same process and add a few layers of petals to finish a bud.

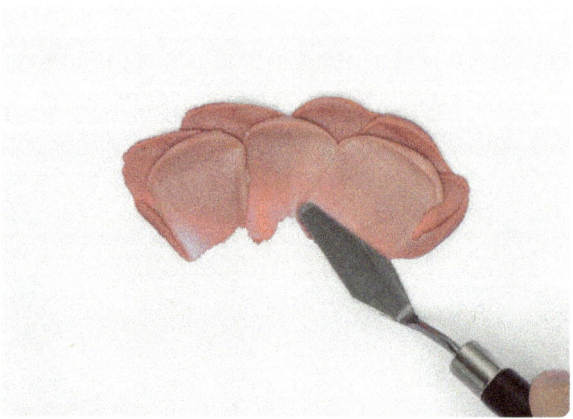

3. For a side-view flower, create the background petals first. Arrange in a semi-circle shape with layers of petals using the side stroke technique (see Basic Strokes)

4. Pipe the center spikes using yellow tinted buttercream in a piping bag with a small hole at the tip.

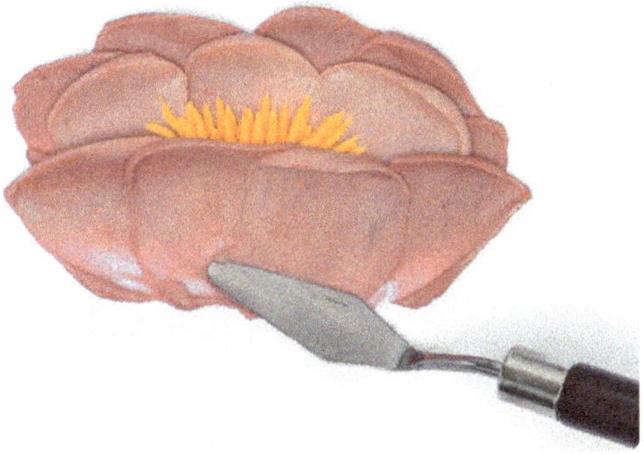

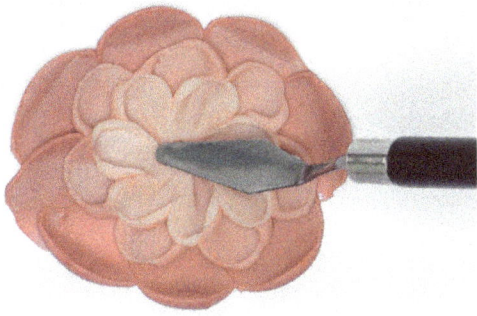

5. Use your palette knife from left to center, right to center, and finally to create the center petal to finish the blossom using the same side stroke.

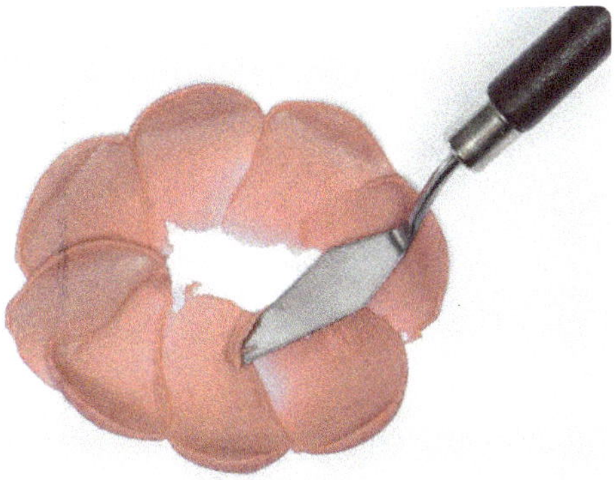

6. For a flat-open view, start with a round of petals of your chosen colour using the same side stroke palette knife painting technique that goes towards the center.

7. Add multiple layers of rounded petals to create a full camellia flower using either press and curve or press and slide technique. Keep an eye on the colour gradient if you are using multiple frosting shades. Each petal has a broader top than bottom. Make a second, lighter layer around the central point to complete the flower.

8. The center part of the flower uses yellow orange tinted buttercream from a small-hole piping bag. Create a pompom of multiple thin spikes.

CAMELLIA | 89

Gardenia

White gardenias are a classic southern flower suitable for wedding cakes, party cakes, and more. The lush frosting technique is as simple as it is beautiful.

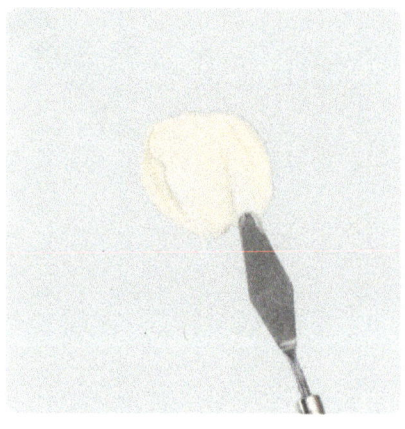

1. Create the beautiful white petals of a gardenia with a large amount of buttercream for the large round shapes using the press and curve stroke. Each petal is made with a press and curve stroke that leaves a slightly curled sculptural shape at the edge. (see Basic Strokes)

2. Create all the petals in a circular shape by turning the palette knife with the handle facing the center as you go. Overlap the edges slightly for a natural look.

3. Add a couple of layers of petals according to your preference or depending on the size of your flower. The petals decrease in size toward the center. Use press and slide stroke to create smaller inner petals.

4. Use a small-hole seamless piping bag to create the bean-shaped yellow center of the flower and the thin dark brown stamen.

5. For side-view gardenia flowers, create the row of petals in the back using press and curve sroke first then pipe the yellow center and stamen pointing against the petals.

6. Finish the front side petals afterward. Do this by starting at the edges and pulling the frosting down toward the center at the bottom.

Tulip

Tulip flowers are a symbol of spring's arrival and are cherished for their beauty and variety. They are known for their vibrant colors and distinctive cup-shaped blossoms. With a few simple strokes, you can create a cake with beautiful tulips in a variety of colours.

1. Use a short, rounded or pointed palette knife with a large amount of frosting to create the bold, cupped petals of the tulip flower. Press, create the slight curve to the side, and then pull downward to finish the first one. (see Basic Strokes)

2. Repeat the same process to create another petal next to it. Make sure the outer edges are neat and thicker than the ones close to each other. The center will be covered up with the third and final petal.

PRO TIP:

Some varieties of tulips have much taller flowers, so you can use a longer palette knife for these petals.

Use slightly different colours or shades for the back and front petal to give a more dimensional look.

3. Then, use the same palette knife technique to make the front petal in the center. This should overlap the side petals quite a bit and form a generally round or oval shape. You can add one or two petals for the front petals

TULIP | 91

Orchid

Orchids come in a wide variety of colours, shapes, and designs, but these classic white ones look simply stunning on any cake. The easy steps and palette knife techniques will help you transform buttercream into an exotic burst of beauty.

1. Use the press and slide stroke with your palette knife to create the three narrow yet rounded petals that form the base of the orchid flower. (see Basic Strokes)

2. Align these in a perfectly triangular shape with one petal pointing straight up and two at 45-degree angles pointing downward.

3. The next two petals are between the side petals and are angled slightly upward like the arms of the star. These are bigger and rounder than the background petals. Use press and curve stroke to get this effect.

4. Lightly press a small amount of pale green frosting to the center of the petals and drag your palette knife to smooth it downward.

5. Start at approximately a 20° angle before turning the knife and lifting it off the flower. This will leave a thicker sculptural element on both sides as seen in the picture. Create the final center lip with a curved bottom.

6. Create the final center lip with a curved bottom.

Sunflower

Big, bold, bright, and beautiful are words that describe the splendour of sunflowers. With a few simple steps, you can recreate these fun flowers in delicious buttercream. They are a favourite for summertime parties and weddings.

1. Use a pointy, narrow-tip palette knife to get the long petals needed for a sunflower. Use the press and slide stroke with bright yellow buttercream for each of the petals. (see Basic Strokes)

2. Repeat the same process to create a row of petals in a circle around a large center point. Turn the palette knife so the handle is pointing inward for each one.

3. Create another set of similar petals on top of the finished base layer. These should be slightly shorter, so the background petals stick out in between each of the points. Fill in the yellow colour to the center in the same way as described in step one.

4. To create the prominent center of the sunflower, push dark brown frosting through a sifter or sieve before arranging it in a circle with a toothpick. (see Dogwood)

5. Do the same thing for very dark green tinted buttercream and fill in the center of this circle. Make sure there are no gaps.

PRO TIP:

Use shading or different orange and yellow tones to create different varieties of sunflowers or give the illusion of more depth. This is especially important for side view flowers.

Make sure the points of the petals in the first and second row do not match up perfectly. They will look more natural if they alternate or overlap in different ways.

SUNFLOWER | 93

Lotus

The lovely lotus blossom symbolizes beauty and serenity. The lush flowers come in a variety of colours to suit any style.

1. Create the many narrow petals of the lotus blossom with a thin-bladed palette knife. Use the press and pull technique. (see Basic Strokes)

2. Place the petals in an arc on one side of the center point. Layer another smaller collection of petals atop the first. Make sure their points do not match up perfectly. For a side-view look, the flower's petals cluster around the top side.

3. Use a small-hole seamless piping bag to pipe the center spikes with a bright yellow-orange tinted buttercream. Pipe them close together but do not create an exceptionally thick mound of buttercream because it will get in the way of the next petal application.

4. Complete the lotus flower with another layer of thin and pointy petals partially covering the center. Be careful not to press too hard and disrupt the design or blend the center and petal colours together.

5. Finish with an arc of petals pointed downward.

PRO TIP:

Use a very pointy palette knife for this project to get the narrow petals that look natural.

Consider using different colours for the lotus blossom as they come in a variety of whites, yellows, and pinks.

For a flat-open look, arrange the layers of petals in a circle (similar to sunflower) and finish off with piped spikes in the center.

Iris

Bearded iris flowers are known for their unique and intricate appearance. They have three upright petals called "standards" that often have a different color or pattern than the three downward-hanging petals called "falls." The falls typically have a prominent fuzzy or "beard" on their inner surface, which gives this iris its name.

1. The large petals of the iris flower are quite wide, so you can use a larger palette knife with a rounded tip for this design. Press and slide technique is used for each petal pointing upwards. (see Basic Strokes)

2. Repeat the same process and arrange these basically parallel to each other and overlapping quite a bit.

3. With the darker frosting colour loaded on your knife, angle the blade to the side and downward. Create a wing-shaped petal on the left at approximately a 45-degree angle.

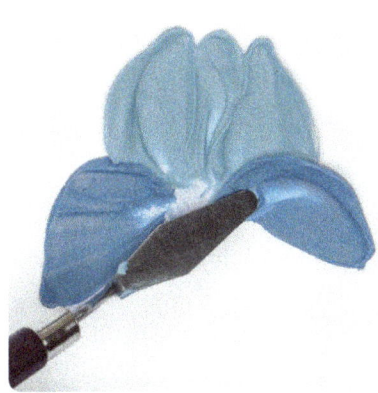

4. Repeat the same technique on the right side so the two petals mirror each other.

5. Create the bottom center petal with the darker frosting using the press and slide knife technique. This is a much broader petal that must cover any gap between the two side ones.

6. Switch to a pointed-tip palette knife loaded with yellow-orange tinted buttercream. Create one narrow accent in the middle of each petal as seen on the image. These represent the prominent pollen-laden beards seen on iris flowers.

IRIS | 95

Marigold

Bright orange brings all the attention to your next cake when you include marigold motifs. These pompom flowers symbolize good luck and happiness and make a wonderful addition to a summer cake design.

1. Use a rounded tip palette knife and press and slide technique to create the many overlapping petals of a brilliant orange marigold flower. Consider blending two or three shades to get a more natural look. (see Basic Strokes)

2. Create an arc of small, round petals for the outer layer. Keep adding layers of slightly smaller petals until you fill in the whole flower shape. Use an arc for a side-view flower.

3. For the side-view flower, add the sepal and stem with dark green tinted buttercream using the same press and slide technique.

4. For a flat-open blossom, arrange the petals in a circle.

5. Repeat the same process and create multiple layers until you fill all the way to the center.

PRO TIP:

Marigolds come in a wide array of warm colours and sizes. Explore photos to get unique combinations. This will help you understand the shapes, colors, and details of marigold petals and leaves.

Scabious

Scabious flowers are dainty and charming with pastel colours and a pinwheel of petals radiating out from the center. They look and smell so sweet in a garden.

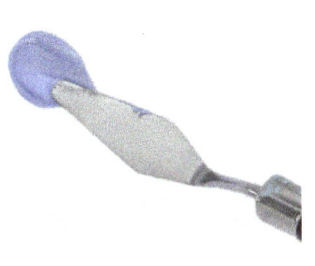

1. For this small-petalled flower, press and slide the palette knife to leave a prominent edge that gives the flower a lovely texture. (see Basic Strokes)

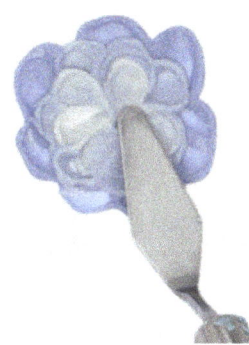

2. A full scabious blossom needs two or three concentric rings of rounded petals in variegated shades of blue. Change from darker to lighter as you add new layers.

3. Add a smear of green buttercream on the center and put the light caramel tinted buttercream on top of it. Create this by pressing frosting through a sieve and arranging it with a toothpick. (see Dogwood)

4. For a scabious flower from the side, create two (or more) layers of petals in a full arc with their tips pointing upward.

5. Add the prominent center part of the scabious flower the same way as discussed on step 3.

6. Finish this side-view flower with one more row of rounded petals pointing upward. These should overlap the center element slightly and come together in a smooth arc at the bottom.

Dahlia

One of the most multi-coloured flower types in the world, dahlias give you many cake decorating options to explore. They also come in sizes from small and dainty to gigantic. You can make your choice from these simple steps.

1. Use a narrow and pointy palette knife and apply the press and slide stroke to create each peaked petal of the dahlia flower. (see Basic Strokes)

2. Repeat the same process and rotate the knife as you go to make a pompom effect with slightly shorter petals at the bottom.

3. With a slightly darker buttercream frosting colour, repeat the first step on top of the existing layer. These petals should be a bit smaller and overlap to leave no empty spaces or gaps.

4. Finish with a final, smaller center layer. In total, a dahlia can have three or four layers of petals.

5. The very center of each flower consists of a dense cluster of spikes of a similar colour to the petals. Continue the narrow petals with your palette knife or use a piping bag to pipe the spikes as seen in the image.

PRO TIP:

Dahlias come in a wide range of colors and patterns, so mix your paint colors accordingly. Consider the colors of the petals, the center details, and any patterns or variations in the flower.

Dahlias often have a darker center surrounded by lighter petals.

Zinnia

A small pompom of variegated colour defines the lovely zinnia flowers. Choose your favourite shade from pink to yellow, orange to white. This is a classic summertime annual perfect for cake decorating designs.

1. Use a round-tipped palette knife to create a ring of neatly spaced petals with your primary buttercream colour. Load your palette knife with a good amount of buttercream and apply press and slide stroke to create each petal. (see Basic Strokes)

2. Add two more layers of petals, each one smaller and lighter than the ones beneath it. This creates a very natural, highlighted effect. Be careful not to press too hard to avoid blending colours or disturbing the shape of the flower.

3. Use a toothpick loaded with a small amount of yellow tinted buttercream to build the textured outer ring of the center element of the flower.

PRO TIP:

The petals on a zinnia are very regular, round, and cupped. Make a side-view flower by layering different shades of buttercream petals in a wide arc. These work well clustered with the full blown blossoms together in a design.

4. Add a dark brown tinted buttercream for the smaller middle mound. Spread the center colour around with a toothpick to make a natural-looking combination of colours.

5. Smear a hint of brown on to the yellow ring for a more realistic look.

Fuchsia

The lovely trailing stems of fuchsia plants carry pink and purple flowers both beautiful and delicate. These symbols of love and beauty are an amazing option for celebration cakes.

1. Build the unique shape of a fuchsia flower starting with the three bottom petals. Use a round-tip palette knife and press and curve stroke for the three rounded shapes clustered together in an overlapping pattern as seen in the image. (see Basic Strokes)

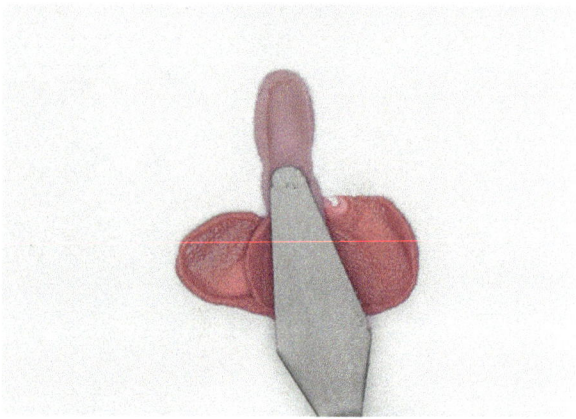

2. Choose the second colour of pink buttercream frosting for the longer, perpendicular tube. Create the elongated petal with the press and slide stroke but longer.

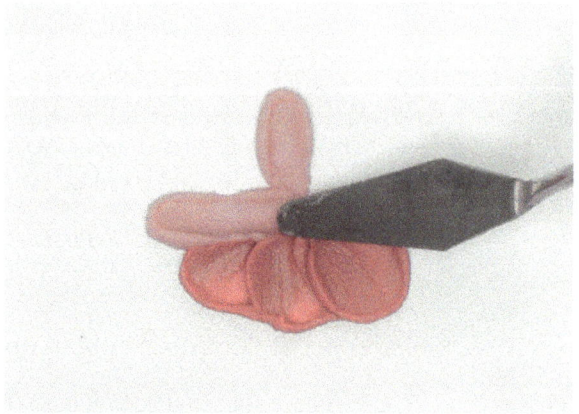

3. Using the same shade of buttercream, add the long sepals. These are the petal-like flower parts that rest over the darker petals at the bottom. Be sure to use enough frosting on your narrow palette knife to build up the slightly dimensional shapes.

4. Repeat the same process to complete about three sepals.

Peony

One of the biggest and boldest flowers in a summer garden is the peony. The large round buds and explosions of colourful petals make a grand impact.

1. Use a broader palette knife to make the large blossoms of the peony flower. Use a combination of press and slide as well as press and curve technique to achieve the frilly petal look. (see Basic Strokes)

2. Repeat the same process and make wide but pointed petals in an arc toward the right. Start with the darkest shade of pink on the left.

3. With the next lightest colour, overlap a row of similar petals from left to right again. Repeat this for a third row with the lightest buttercream shade.

4. Use a seamless piping bag with a small hole to pipe the yellow-orange stamen in a tight cluster together in the center of the petal arc.

5. Finish the side-view peony flower with three rows of similar petals. Start with the lightest colour overlapping the center stamens slightly then use the middle pink shade to overlap those lightest colour petals.

6. Finally, create three darker petals from the sides before finishing with a broad center petal at the bottom using side stroke technique. (see Basic Strokes)

Rose

No other flower means as much as the rose. This classic favourite means romance, beauty, and peace depending on the colours chosen. Recreate buds and blossoms in delicious buttercream frosting.

1. Start with the smallest and simplest rosebud. Use a pointy palette knife with press and slide and press and curve strokes to create three off-set layers of buttercream in a curved oval shape. Retain the thicker top edges of the petals to indicate the classic tightly furled shape of the bud. (see Basic Strokes)

2. For a larger bud, start with a rounded dab of buttercream at the top with a side stroke technique. (see Basic Strokes)

3. Load the tip of your palette knife with a small amount of buttercream to swirl this into a rough spiral or series of rings to indicate the cluster of petals inside.

4. Load the palette knife with more buttercream for the two outer petals. Move the knife in a gentle arc from left to the center.

5. Repeat the same process to do the right side, overlapping the edges of the foreground petals. Do not cover the swirl you made in step two completely.

6. The side-view rose starts with few press and slide and side stroke wider petals at either side near the bottom of the flower shape and a lot of the side stroke petals for the rounded base layer of petals.

7. Repeat this technique for all additional layers working your way toward the center. Always work in a circular motion instead of a basic arc like with other flower types. Use photos of real roses for inspiration.

8. Finish with broad, side stroke petals at the bottom before adding foliage.

9. For a flat open rose, the process is quite a bit different. Instead of starting on the outer edge, you begin in the middle with a series of curved press and pull petals surrounding a central point.

10. Repeat the same process and make the petals larger as you make more layers. Overlap these petals slightly to avoid unattractive gaps.

11. Complete the full rose according to the size you require. The last petal usually will have an excess but it can easily be removed and shaped with a clean palette knife.

PRO TIP:

To enhance the three-dimensional effect, add highlights using lighter colors and shadows using darker colors. Use the palette knife to apply these highlights and shadows to the raised areas of the petals.

Vary the pressure and angle of the knife to create different textures and contours.

Ranunculus

The tight spirals of ranunculus petals make for an amazing cake decoration display when carefully placed with your palette knife. Try this symbol of charm and grace in your favourite shades of pink, yellow, white, or red.

1. For a side-view flower version, begin the back wide petals using the side stroke technique. Hold your knife sideways and pull down toward where the flower center will be. (see Basic Strokes)

2. Add a second layer of lighter petals directly over these.

3. Create the large center of the ranunculus flower with a circle of light green frosting with a slightly smaller dark green circle on top.

4. Add the bottom layers of broad side stroke petals. These should overlap the center green element slightly and pull down toward the bottom. Use lighter frosting for the inner petals.

5. Repeat the same process and use a darker shade of orange for the final layer.

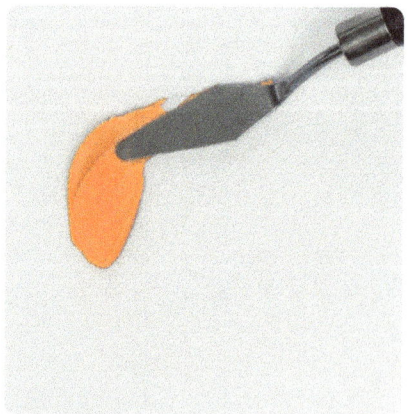

6. A full blossom is crafted in the round much like a rose, but this one starts at the outer edge and works toward the center instead. Use a combination of curved press and curve and side strokes for the petals.

7. Turn your palette knife as you create multiple layers of petals that overlap until you fill in the gap.

8. Repeat the same process and overlap a row of similar petals with the next lighter shade.

9. As the space in the center becomes smaller, you will have to use a combination of press and curve and side strokes to add the layers of petals. This will require less movement, thus less chances of damaging the other petals.

PRO TIP:

Use the palette knife to create the texture of the petals. Swipe and dab the knife to mimic the petal shapes. Vary the pressure and angles to achieve a dimensional effect.

Ranunculus flowers come in a variety of colors, so feel free to choose a palette that resonates with your artistic vision.

You can add more texture and depth to the background using the palette knife. Consider creating contrast between the detailed flowers and a more abstract background.

10. Complete the ranunculus flower with the same center design. Use a light green center topped with a darker green one.

Summer Garden

Create a cacophony of colour across this stunning flower cake with simple palette knife painting techniques. Iris, sunflowers, daisies, poppies, and more cover the towering tiers in a rainbow of hues.

You will need

Tools:
- palette knife
- piping bags

Cake:
- Top tier: Round cake, 15cm (6in) X 15cm (6in) high
- Bottom tier: Round cake, 20cm (8in) X 20cm (8in) high

Buttercream:
- 1.2kg (42oz) white for crumb coating and final cover
- 150gms (5.3oz) dark green
- 100gms (3.5oz) light green
- 150gms (5.3oz) red
- 100gms (3.5oz) white
- 100gms (3.5oz) light violet
- 100gms (3.5oz) dark violet
- 100gms (3.5oz) light pink
- 100gms (3.5oz) dark pink
- 100gms (3.5oz) orange
- 100gms (3.5oz) Yellow
- 100gms (3.5oz) light blue

1. Start with the long, outermost leaves using a large quantity of buttercream frosting on your pointed palette knife.

2. Add fuchsia flowers trailing to the sides and bottom edge and blue iris buds with overlapping green cups and stems in an appropriate design pointing toward the center of the empty cake surface.

3. Arrange three large iris flowers as seen in the image. These should overlap the leaves, stems, and smaller buds and flowers to a slight degree. Be careful not to press hard or pull the lower layers of buttercream frosting to avoid mixing colours.

4. Add dark green sunflower leaves and use a toothpick to add the veins.

5. Add some daisies and sunflowers in varying sizes and positions. Overlap some details for a natural look.

6. Continue decorating with the bottom tier of the cake with an assortment of other beautiful poppies. Make sure to use thicker buttercream for the leaves that would go over the petals to avoid colour bleed-through.

7. Next, add clusters of dogwood flowers over their light green leaves right at the bottom part of the cake. Notice the position of the leaves as they are all pointing down.

8. Add the beautiful pansies in varying sizes, colours and positions. Finally, add the stamen in the center of each pansy with a black tinted buttercream in a piping bag.

Floral Symphony

On a backdrop of summer sky-tinged buttercream, an assortment of colourful flowers cascade over this two-tiered cake. Lovely lavender, bold zinnias, sunny marigolds, and more arc in a spray of beauty that mimics the perfect summer garden.

You will need

Tools:
- palette knife
- piping bags

Cake:
- Top tier: Round cake, 15cm (6in) X 15cm (6in) high
- Bottom tier: Round cake, 20cm (8in) X 20cm (8in) high

Buttercream:
- 1.2kg (42oz) white for crumb coating and final cover
- 150gms (5.3oz) dark green
- 100gms (3.5oz) light green
- 150gms (5.3oz) red
- 100gms (3.5oz) white
- 100gms (3.5oz) light violet
- 100gms (3.5oz) dark violet
- 100gms (3.5oz) light pink
- 100gms (3.5oz) dark pink
- 100gms (3.5oz) orange
- 100gms (3.5oz) Yellow
- 100gms (3.5oz) light blue

1. Load your palette knife with a large quantity of green buttercream for the background leaves. Press and slide multiple long shapes arranged in a natural progression on the top and bottom tier of the cake. Use a lightly blended buttercream with purple, blue, and similar natural lavender colours to make the stalks. Each one is made up of many small, rounded buds or petal shapes.

2. Add the jasmine flowers throughout the cake and then the bright marigolds. Add more lavenders in between the leaves and other spaces. These are the background floral elements for the overall multi-flower design, so make them first before adding the larger flowers.

3. Add the large anthurium flowers. Use a blended pink and red to create a realistic look.

4. Add the leaves on the anthurium flowers. Since the flower uses a deep colour, make sure to use a thick amount of buttercream for the leaves to avoid colour bleed-through. Use a small-hole seamless piping bag to add the textured dots in the center (spadix) of each of the anthurium. Add more filler flowers like jasmine as desired.

5. Add the zinnias in varying sizes and positions.

6. Finally add the beautiful dahlias. It will be normal for this flower to overlap other elements surrounding it.

FLORAL SYMPHONY | 109

Bountiful Blooms

Imagine a secret garden full of enchanting blooms, and you will get a great idea of how impressive this palette knife cake truly is. Delicate white orchids hang across the top tier as brilliant ranunculus and scabious flowers provide a pleasing contrast. Serene lotus blossoms float beneath to finish out this exotic garden design.

You will need

Tools:
- palette knife
- piping bags

Cake:
- Top tier: Round cake, 15cm (6in) X 10cm (4in) high
- Middle tier: Round cake, 20cm (8in) X 15cm (6in) high
- Bottom tier: Round cake, 25cm (10in) X 10cm (4in) high

Buttercream:
- 1.4kg (50oz) light grey for crumb coating and final cover
- 60gms (2.1oz) dark grey
- 150gms (5.3oz) white
- 150gms (5.3oz) light yellow
- 100gms (3.5oz) dark yellow
- 150gms (5.3oz) dark green
- 150gms (5.3oz) light green
- 100gms (3.5oz) light orange
- 100gms (3.5oz) dark orange
- 150gms (5.3oz) dark pink
- 60gms (2.1oz) light blue
- 60gms (2.1oz) dark blue

BOUNTIFUL BLOOMS | 110

1. Focus on the top tier first with a scattered collection of pretty white orchids. Use a piping bag to create the green stems and a round-tipped palette knife for a few darker green buds or leaves.

2. On the second tier, start by adding gorgeous tulip blooms. Use a blend of pinks and some oranges. Use medium green tinted buttercream on a small-hole seamless piping bag to pipe the stems.

3. Insert some long and light green leaves in between the tulips. Intentionally overlap some of them for a more natural look.

4. Arrange a spread of big and bright orange ranunculus. Create both side-view and full-bloom flowers of this variety to give the cake even more points of interest.

5. Fill in the bottom edge of the second tier with small, blue scabious flowers. The orange and blue colour scheme is highly complementary and eye-catching.

6. On the bottom tier of the cake, start with the unique, broad leaves of the lotus. Use a toothpick to add the intricate leaf veins.

7. Add the beautiful lotus blossoms. Let the edges of the bud and main flower extend slightly beyond the top of this cake tier for a unique sculptural effect. Remember to make the background elements first and layer the big flowers on top.

8. Finally, add the stems and other details with a piping bag.

Rose Soirée

This glorious multi-tier cake highlights the beauty of red roses atop a riotous medley of other brilliant blooms. Yellow freesia, purple violets, blue hydrangea and white gardenia blend together atop the blue marbled background to make a truly impressive cake design.

You will need

Tools:
- palette knife
- piping bags

Cake:
- Top tier: Round cake, 15cm (6in) X 15cm (6in) high
- Bottom tier: Round cake, 20cm (8in) X 10cm (4in) high

Buttercream:
- 1kg (35.2oz) turquoise for crumb coating and final cover
- 150gms (5.3oz) red
- 150gms (5.3oz) white
- 150gms (5.3oz) dusky pink
- 100gms (3.5oz) dark green
- 100gms (3.5oz) light green
- 100gms (3.5oz) light blue
- 100gms (3.5oz) dark blue
- 100gms (3.5oz) light yellow
- 100gms (3.5oz) dark violet
- 60gms (2.1oz) dark brown

1. Begin at the top of the cake with broad green leaves in the background first. Use a toothpick to sketch in the leaf veins for added detail. Create a couple tightly furled rose buds in a red and pink shade.

2. Overlap additional leaves and a full rose flower prominently placed on the top tier. Also, add a side-view rose near the base that overlaps some of the bottom petals of the main flower.

3. Fill in the space beside the roses with delicate yellow freesia flowers before moving on to the lower cake tier.

4. With the leaves created first in the background, continue the full bouquet collection with white gardenia.

5. Add a beautiful cluster of violets as they cascade over the edges between the first and second tier of the cake. Use a toothpick or a small-hole piping bag to apply or pipe the bright yellow center of each of the blossoms.

6. Map out the shapes of the hydrangea flowers using different shades of blue. Remember the use of shadow effects to create gorgeous texture and depth.

7. Add the pink camellia buds and open blossoms. Incorporate both side-view and flat-open flowers to enhance the overall look of this cake.

8. Lastly, add the stems and other fine details of the camellia with a piping bag.

ROSE SOIREE

3 Dimensional

This three dimensional palette knife painting technique (also known as impasto technique) is known for its textured and bold appearance, as the palette knife allows artists to create quite thick, impasto layers of paint that can result in a dynamic and realistic visual effect.

Techniques

We highly suggest to use any thick type of frosting or chocolate ganache for this technique to be effective. The strokes and textures used are deliberately left visible. This allows the artist to showcase their technique and style more prominently.

Sunflower

Bright, happy sunflowers get a unique look with this 3D sculptural design using simple palette knife techniques. These yellow blooms are popular for summertime cakes. Use the Queen of Hearts crusting buttercream for the best results.

Pointy Petal - Style 1

1. The pointed petal stroke for sculptured flower design is quite similar to the technique used in flat palette knife painting. However, instead of holding the knife flat and parallel to the surface of the cake, you tilt it up so the point angles away from the cake. This means the bulk of the buttercream frosting will remain on the surface instead of being smoothed flat or remaining on the knife. As you slide the knife to the base of the petal, it angles closer to the surface to thin the dimensional aspect.

2. Use a greater volume of frosting for each individual petal than you would for 2D painting. Slide the knife at an angle downward toward the center as you lay the yellow buttercream out in the correct shape for the first petal. Repeat this process around in a circle to make the sunflower.

3D - SUNFLOWER | 116

3. Adjust petal tip angles slightly as needed with the clean end of a palette knife. Gently and carefully manipulate the position of the petals. This ensures that the elements will not collapse or get out of shape from any overlapping petals.

4. Push a small amount of dark brown buttercream through a sieve or sifter for the natural dotted look for the center of the flower. Repeat the same process for the green center.

5. Use a toothpick to position it naturally in the middle of the sunflower.

Sunflowers come in a variety of sizes. Choose three, four, or even more layers of petals to create a unique look.

You can give a little time until the layers have slightly crusted before manipulating the angle and/or position of the petals.

Sunflowers are known for their bright yellow petals and rich brown centers. A sunflower painting would typically incorporate these colors, but artists may also add variations or use contrasting colors to create visual interest.

Lotus

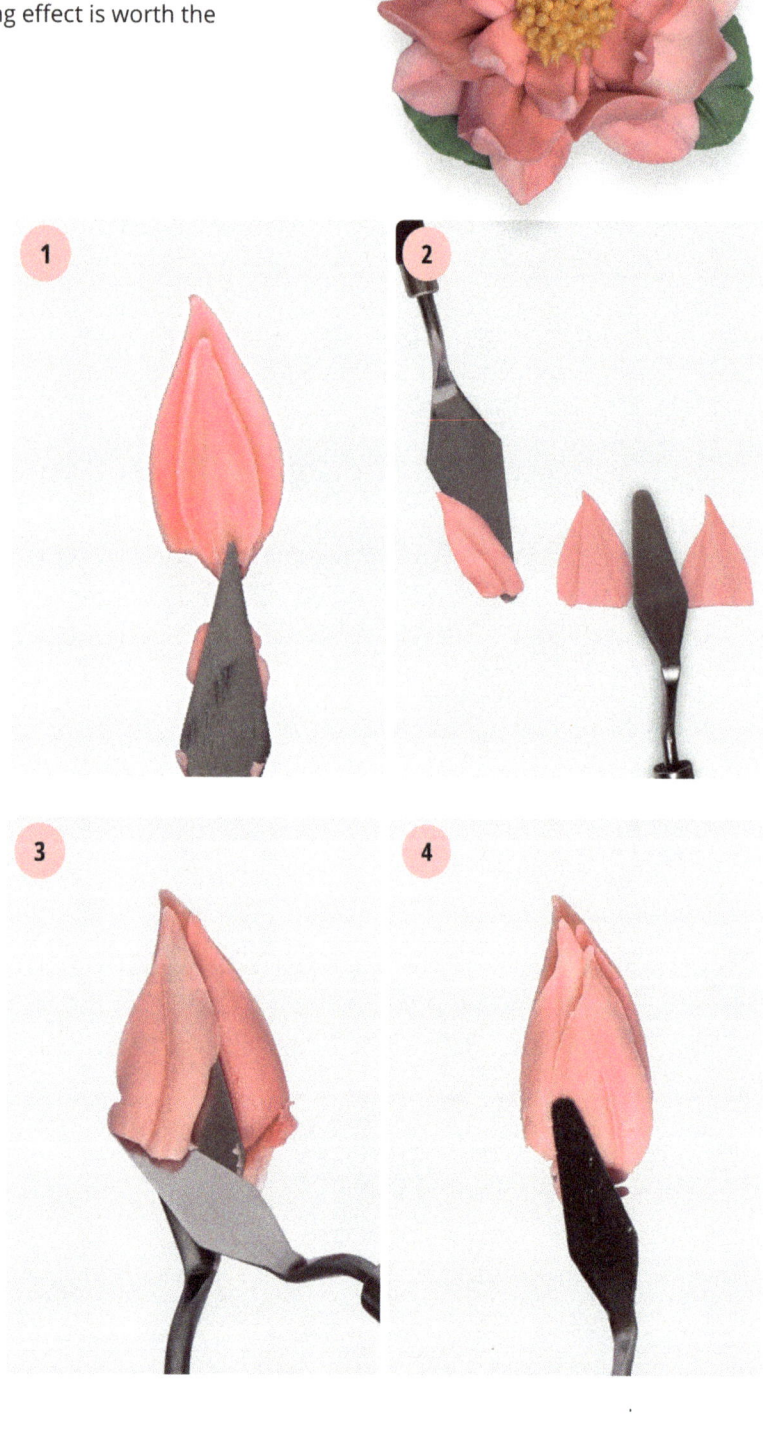

Carefully layered petals in a variety of pretty pink shades bright these 3D lotus blossoms to life for your next cake. While a bit more challenging than flat flower designs, the stunning effect is worth the effort.

Pointy Petal - Style 2

1. Using the press and slide stroke with a pointy pallette knife, create overlapping petals to give volume to the lotus bud.

2. On a separate working board, create a couple of pointy petals. When the petal is slightly crusted, quickly slide the palette knife underneath the petal to detach it from the surface. Depending how you will arrange the petal, decide whether to position the palette knife with its tip parallel to the tip of the petal or pointed to the base.

3. Position the petal accordingly then use another palette to help slide the petal off the main palette knife. Use the palette knife to cut any excess buttercream or shape it accordingly.

4. Repeat the same process and add as many petals as needed. Bring some of the petals lower then the others to make it more realistic.

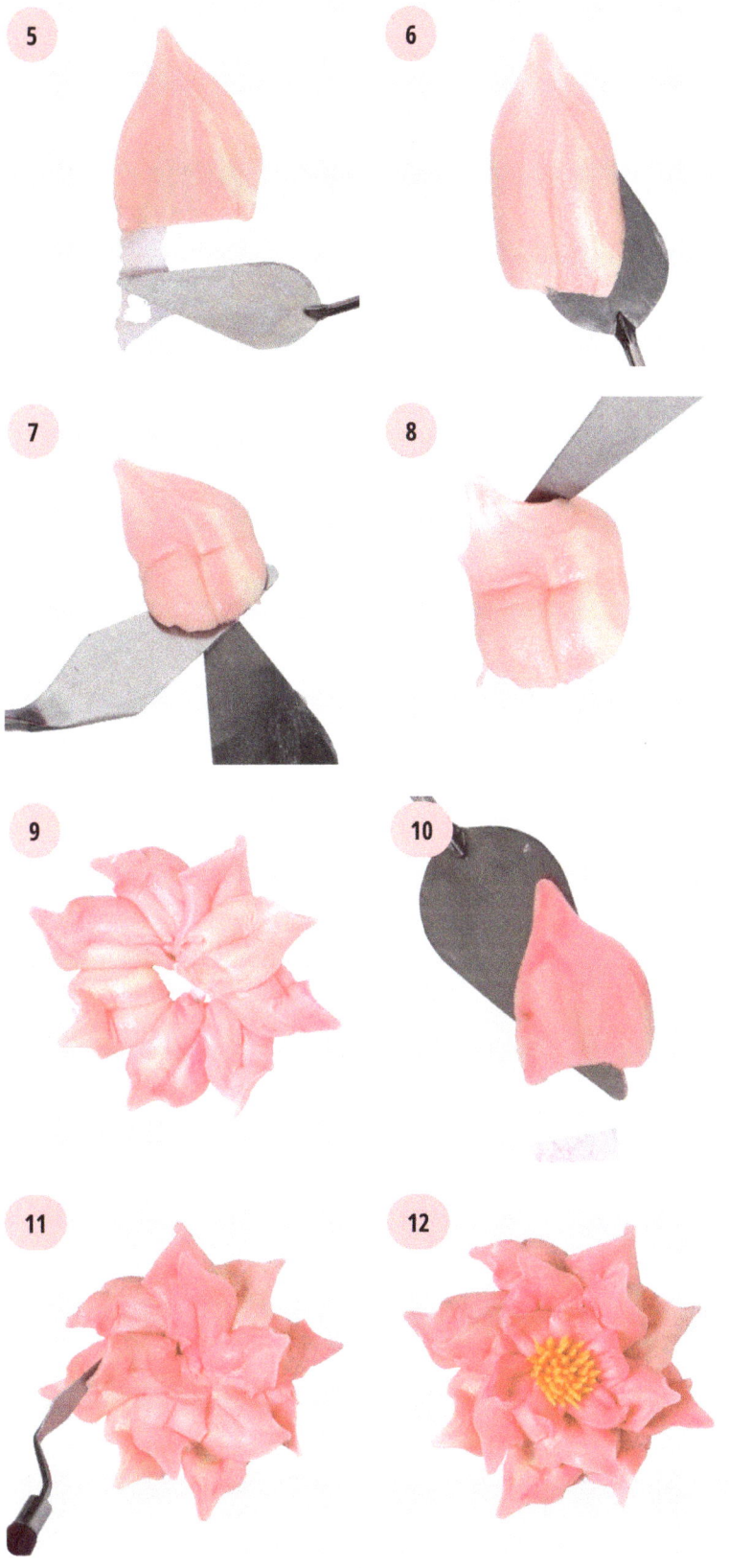

5. Create individual petals using a wide, pointed palette knife and a large quantity of blended buttercream frosting. Press and slide to create the wide petal. Cut the base of each petal off in a straight line to maintain a wide base.

6. Slide the palette knife under the petal to detach it from the surface. Be careful not to squash the petal. Cutting the base off helps prevent this problem.

7. Position your petal then use another clean palette knife to slide the petal off your main palette knife.

8. Gently pinch or manipulate these to give them natural looking shapes and bends.

9. Position the finished petals in a circle around an open center space to create the first layer of the lotus flower.

10. For the final inner layer of petals, cut the original shapes shorter and bend them slightly more when arranging them in the circle around the center point of the flower. Slide the palette knife the other way around as it would be easier to position the petals that way.

11. Position and manipulate the petals as needed.

12. Create the center stamen cluster of the lotus flower using yellow-orange buttercream in a seamless piping bag.

Dogwood

With simple 3D sculpting techniques, a palette knife, and a simple toothpick, you can create dogwood blossoms so realistic they look like they came right off the tree. These fresh springtime flowers look lovely when combined with other colourful options.

Rounded Petal - Style 1

1. Start by creating enough press and slide petals with a rounded palette knife for all the dogwood flowers you plan to use on the cake. Use a good amount of frosting for each as the petals even though they are quite small. This ensures that you will be able to maintain their shape.

2. Use the edge of a clean palette knife to cut off the lower, thinner edge of all the petals in a straight line to maintain a wide base.

3. After waiting a short while for the buttercream to crust, quickly slide the palette knife under the petal to detach it from the surface. Be careful not to squash the petal. Cutting the base off helps prevent this problem.

When detaching the petals from the surface, make sure to position the petal just at the tip of the palette knife for ease of removing later.

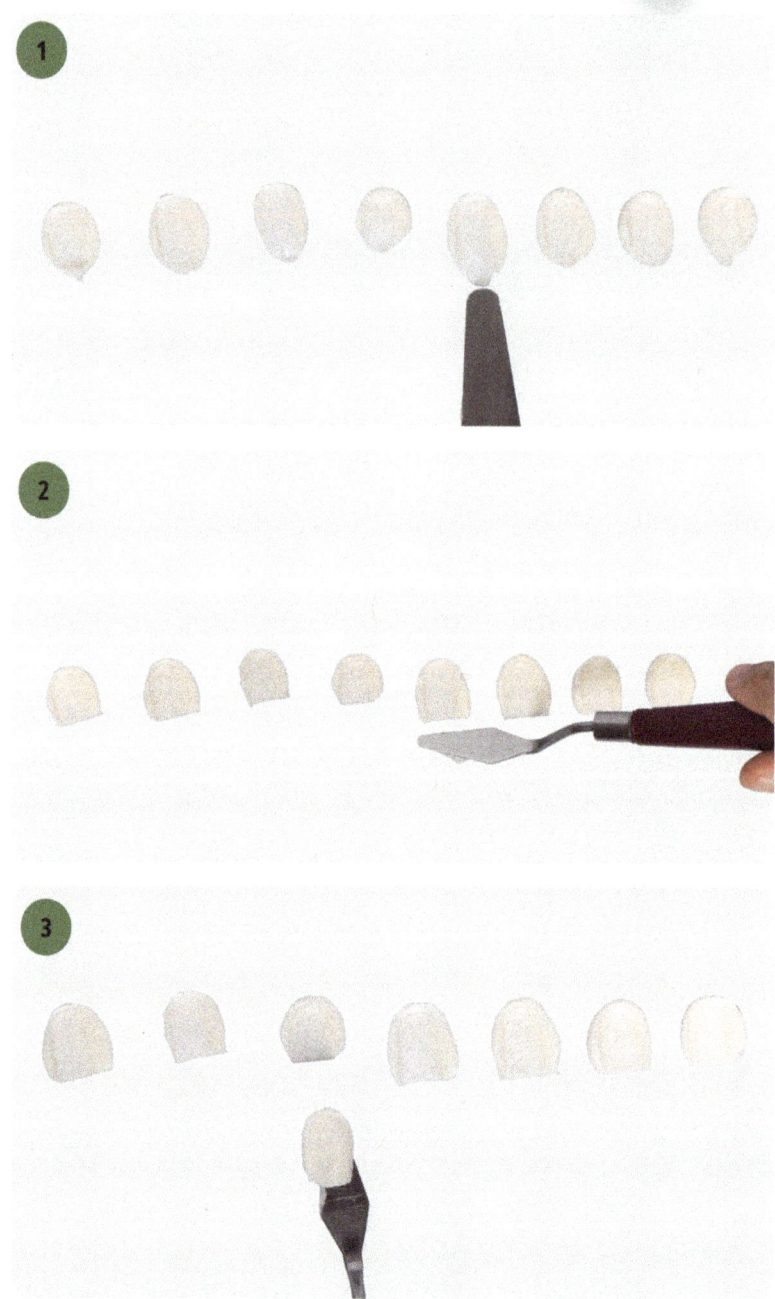

4. Use another palette knife to help release the petal off the main palette knife.

5. Arrange a group of four white petals for each dogwood flower.

6. Use the small tip of a palette knife to cut out a tiny divot in the center of each petal. Hold the petal up with another knife while you do this to prevent pressing too hard and flattening the petal to the surface. Alternatively, you can do this process before you lift the petal off the board. However, you risk of losing the divot as it could get squashed due to movement.

7. With a light caramel colour frosting in a seamless piping bag, trace a thin line around the edge of each of these divots in the petals.

8. Pass a small amount of light green buttercream frosting through a sieve to create the textured center. Position this carefully with a toothpick. (see Dogwood)

Start by collecting reference images of dogwood flowers. Look for images that show the flowers in different stages of blooming, as well as the overall structure of the tree.

Plan your composition before you start painting. Decide on the placement of the flowers, branches, and leaves within the canvas. Consider factors like balance, focal points, and negative space.

Dogwood flowers come in various shades, including white, pink, and red. Choose a color palette that complements the flowers while also capturing the natural lighting and environment.

Hydrangea

Create a realistic hydrangea cluster from sweet blue buttercream with this unique palette knife technique. This popular flower for summertime decorating is easier to create than it looks. Try the same blossom in white, pink, or pale purple for unique designs.

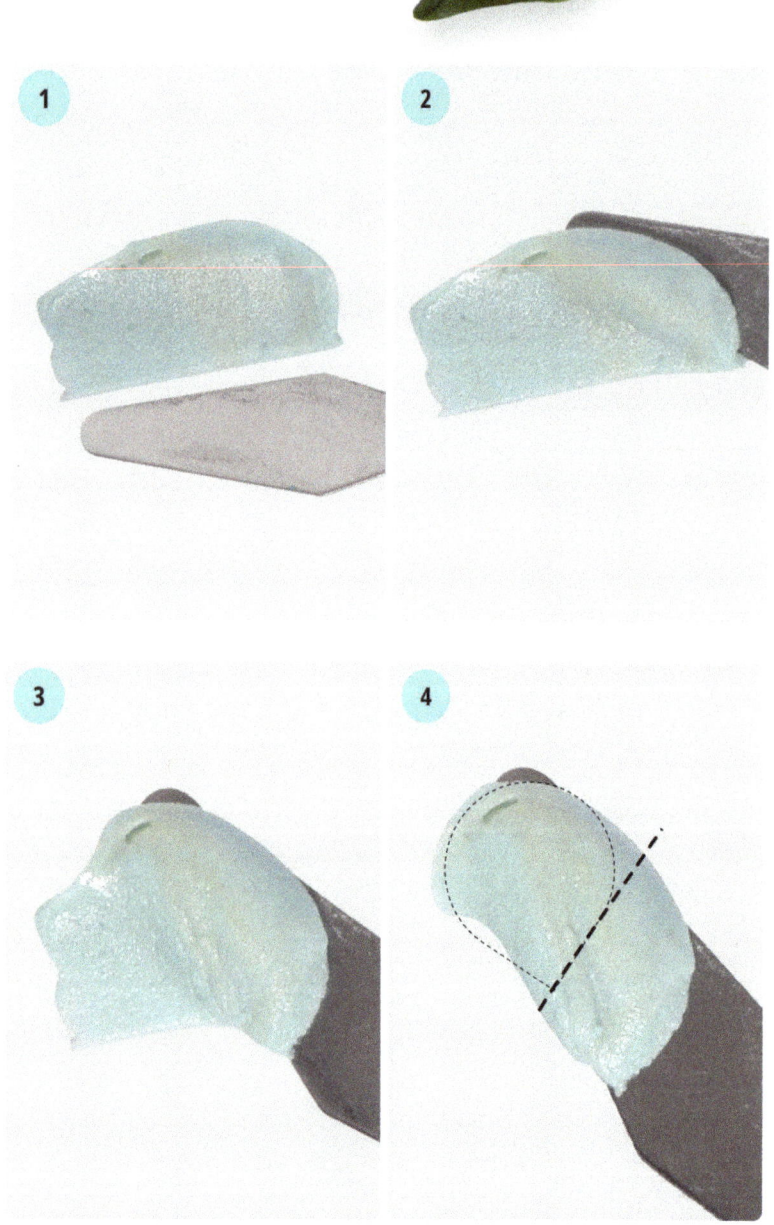

Rounded Petal - Style 2

1. Load a narrow palette knife with a smooth mound of buttercream frosting. Make sure it does not distend over the edges or you risk making an unattractive edge to each hydrangea petal. Use the side stroke to create the petal and slice the bottom edge of the buttercream off in a straight line. The remaining frosting should be wider than it is tall.

2. Use your clean palette knife to gently lift the petal off the surface starting from one edge. Slide the palette knife under the petal starting from one end and move to the side while gently gathering the frosting into a rounded shape.

3. Turn the knife blade as you go to create a wider curve on the top and a narrower bottom edge.

4. Use a second palette knife to gently shape or cut the edges of the base of the petal to get a "V" shape so they are easier to put together.

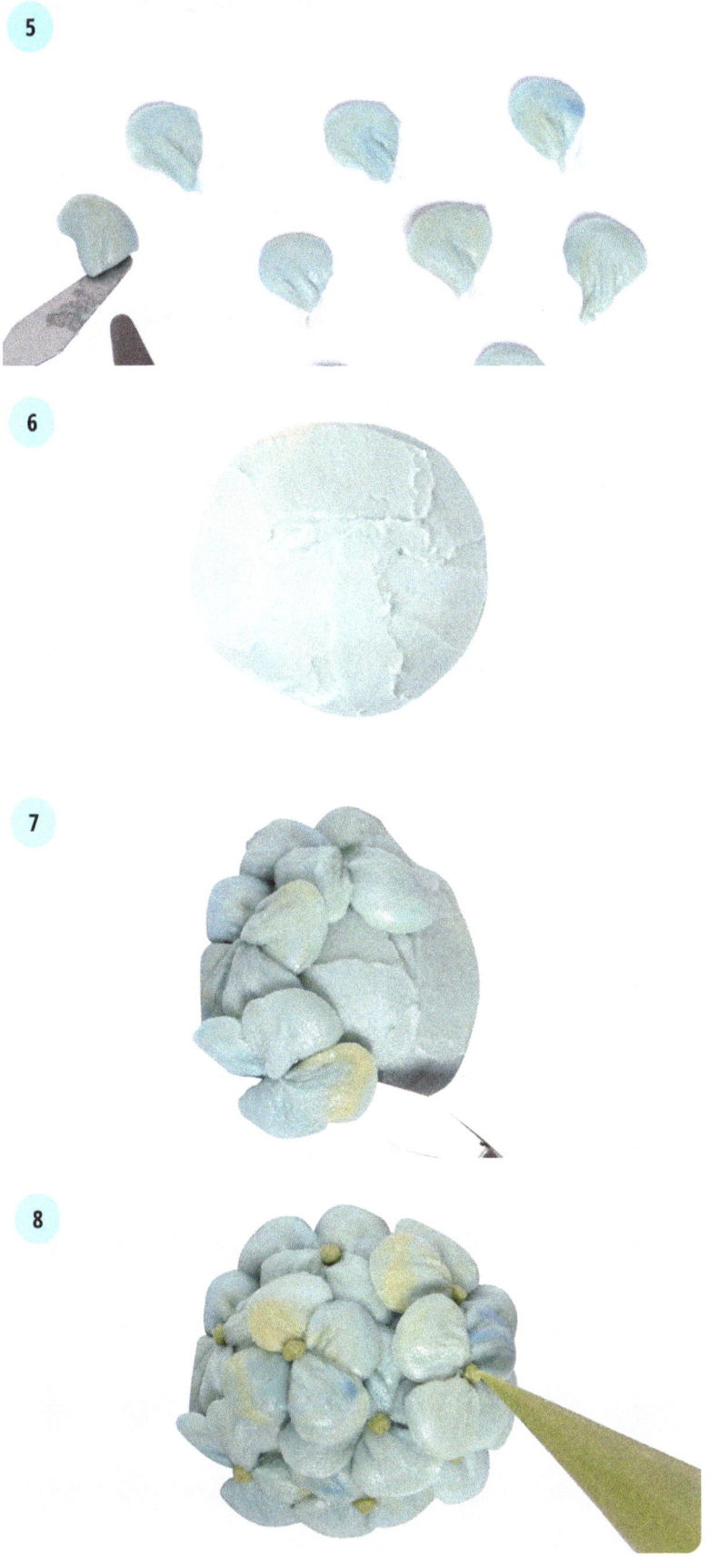

5. Slide the resulting petal off the knife onto the work surface or the cake directly. As each hydrangea cluster has a lot of individual flowers with four petals each, it is a good idea to create them separately on a board instead of on the cake itself. This gives you more time to perfect the petals before building the end design. Make as many buttercream petals as you need to complete the floral decoration. Each should have a slightly sculptural rounded top edge and a narrow, gathered bottom edge.

6. Build a dome or mound of the same color buttercream. This provides the three-dimensional platform for the hydrangea cluster.

7. Arrange the petals you already made in clusters of four to make the individual flowers. Start at the bottom of the mound and work your way to the top center.

8. Finish off this beautiful design with a seamless piping bag loaded with pale green buttercream. Pipe a small dot in the center of each cluster of four petals to complete the natural look.

For hydrangeas, you'll likely need shades of blue, purple, pink, or even white, depending on the variety that you like. Mix your desired colors on the palette, trying to capture the various tones and highlights you see in your reference image.

Add shadows and highlights to the petals and leaves to give them depth and dimension. Observe your reference image to see where the light is hitting the blooms and replicate that on your painting.

Step back and assess your painting. Make any necessary adjustments to colors, shapes, and details. Don't be afraid to make changes to achieve the desired effect.

3D - HYDRANGEA | 123

Peony

A rigid petal lifelike peony creates a big impact in buttercream frosting. The unique colour-blending method creates impressive flowers that look a lot more challenging to make than they really are.

Rigid Cut Petal

1. Prepare the base colour of buttercream frosting first with a plain or gradient of different shades layered together. Create your own blends with natural peony shades like white, pink and yellow.

2. Hold the palette knife perpendicular to the buttercream on the work surface to make the rigid cut petal. With short, quick strokes, scrape very small amounts of the frosting onto the knife one after the other. These small layers will pile up into curved petal shape with distinct ridges over the surface.

The thick layers of buttercream applied on the the palette knife can add a sense of depth and three-dimensionality to the artwork, as the texture created by the knife strokes can mimic the natural texture of the flower petals.

3. Pipe a guide circle with a thin line of frosting to make it easy to arrange the petals for this large flower. Apply the first petal from the palette knife with the textured part down toward the surface.

4. Complete the entire circle by alternating the petal directions to create an irregular and more natural three-dimensional look.

5. Prepare the succeeding row of petals. Create some that curl on the side for a more dimensional look. You can achieve this by doing more short strokes so buttercream will pile up more.

6. Lift each petal from the top side. Picking up the petal from the top would make it easier to position the petals and avoid damaging the other petals.

7. Position them while carefully preserving the thicker or slightly curled sides. Use two clean knives to affix the petals to the flower while maintaining spaces between them.

8. You can also position the petals as normal but be careful not squash the ones beneath.

9. Use the tip of your palette knife to manipulate the position or angle of petals as necessary.

10. Create the yellow center of the sculptured peony flower using a seamless piping bag. Create multiple tightly packed stamen pointing straight upward together.

11. Make several more petals as described in the previous steps. This time, cut the bottoms off much shorter so they fit snugly around the yellow center element.

12. Once these petals develop a slight crust, carefully arrange them in an open-topped cup around the stamens. They should overlap slightly on all sides for the most natural design. If they do not naturally cave in as seen in the photo, gently push with your palette knife to get the desired look.

3D - PEONY | 125

13. The side-view sculptured peony flower is constructed using the same types of petals that were described above. Create many right away with your marbled buttercream frosting in an arc.

14. Repeat the same process and create two or more layers of arced petals.

15. Use the piping bag to pile a thick collection of yellow-orange stamen spikes.

16. The petals that go over the center element can have either the smooth or textured surface of the petals facing outward. The textured side looks a bit more natural as this shows the underside of the petals.

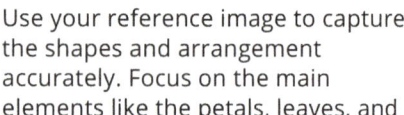

Use your reference image to capture the shapes and arrangement accurately. Focus on the main elements like the petals, leaves, and stems.

Start with the base color of the petals and then layer on darker and lighter shades to create depth and dimension. Pay attention to the curves and folds of the petals to make them look realistic.

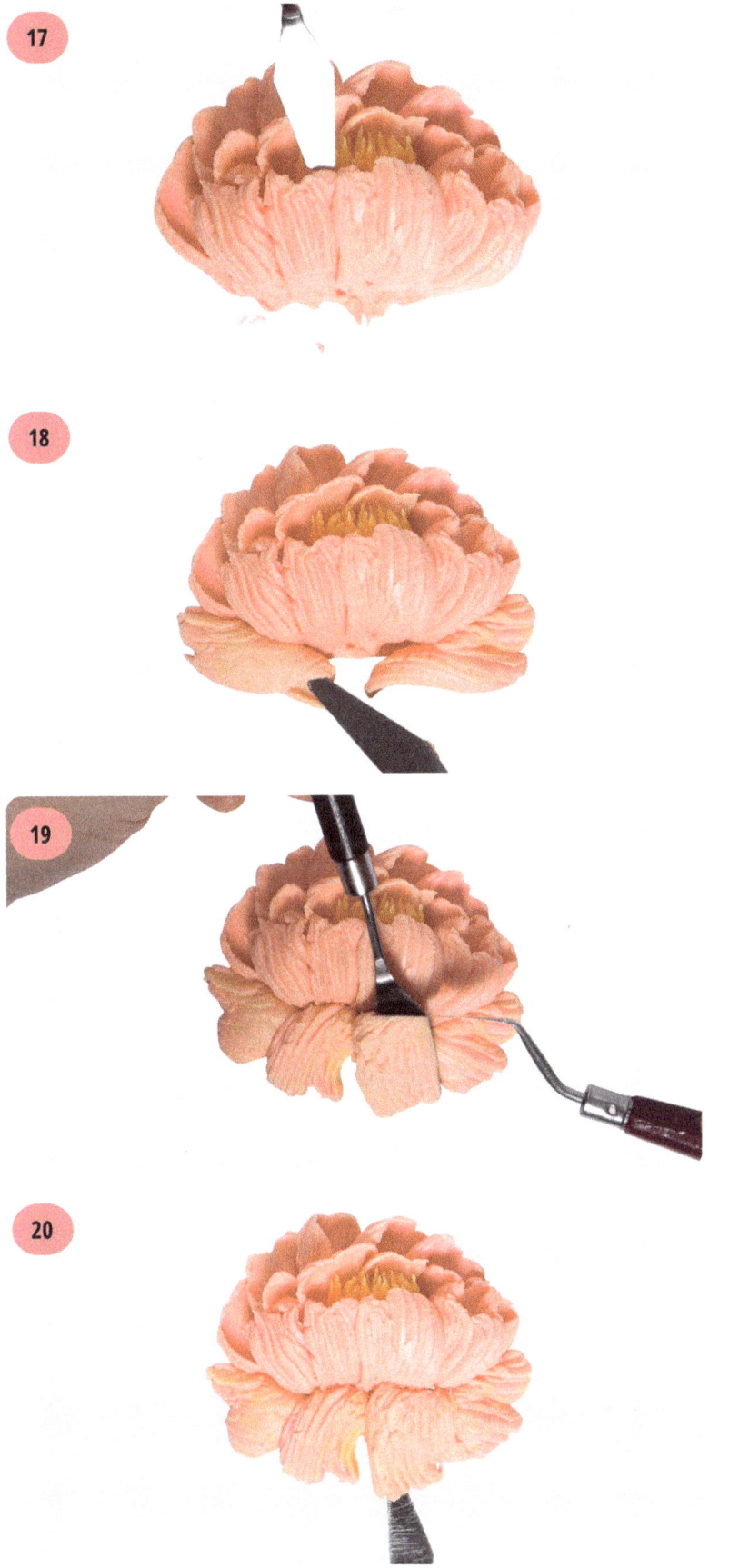

17. Use the tip of your palette knife to manipulate the position or angle of petals as necessary.

18. Add a few broad petals at the very bottom of the blossom pointing downward away from the bulk of the peony flower. Start with some petals on the left and right.

19. Add two or more petals directed basically straight down to finish the design.

20. Use the tip of the palette knife to adjust the angle or position of the petals.

Experiment with color mixing, layering, and texture in unique ways, creating visually striking and expressive artworks.

Choose a clear and detailed reference image of peonies. This will help you understand the structure, colors, and details of the flowers. Apply various colors of tinted buttercream to create the different elements of the flower, such as petals, leaves, and stems.

You can also lightly sketch the outline of the peonies on your cake using a toothpick or a cocktail stick. Focus on the main shapes of the petals, leaves, and stems.

Orchid

Elegant white orchid flowers make beautiful accents for cake decorating. Use your palette knife and the techniques you already learned to create these exotic blossoms from sweet buttercream.

Two-Stroke Petal - Style 1

1. Create the two-stroke petal by first making a sided stroke petal with the white frosting. Maintain a thicker, curved ridge on the right or left that will become the edges of each petal. Use the palette knife edge to cut off the thinnest edge of buttercream opposite the curved side. Repeat the same process for the opposite petal.

2. Carefully pick up one side petal and arrange it next to the opposite side. The cut edges form the seam in the center of the single large petal. If they do not stick together, use the tip of your palette knife or a rounded paintbrush to run it on the center to gently join them together.

3. Lift the joined petal carefully and position then release with a help of another palette knife.

4. Create three long petals and arrange them in the design shown here. These are actually the sepals of the orchid flower.

5. Make a long side stroke petal from buttercream that covers the whole length of the palette knife and cut the thin edge of the petal. (see rounded patal - style 2)

6. Turn the palette knife gently as you go to create a wide curved petal shape.

3D - ORCHID | 128

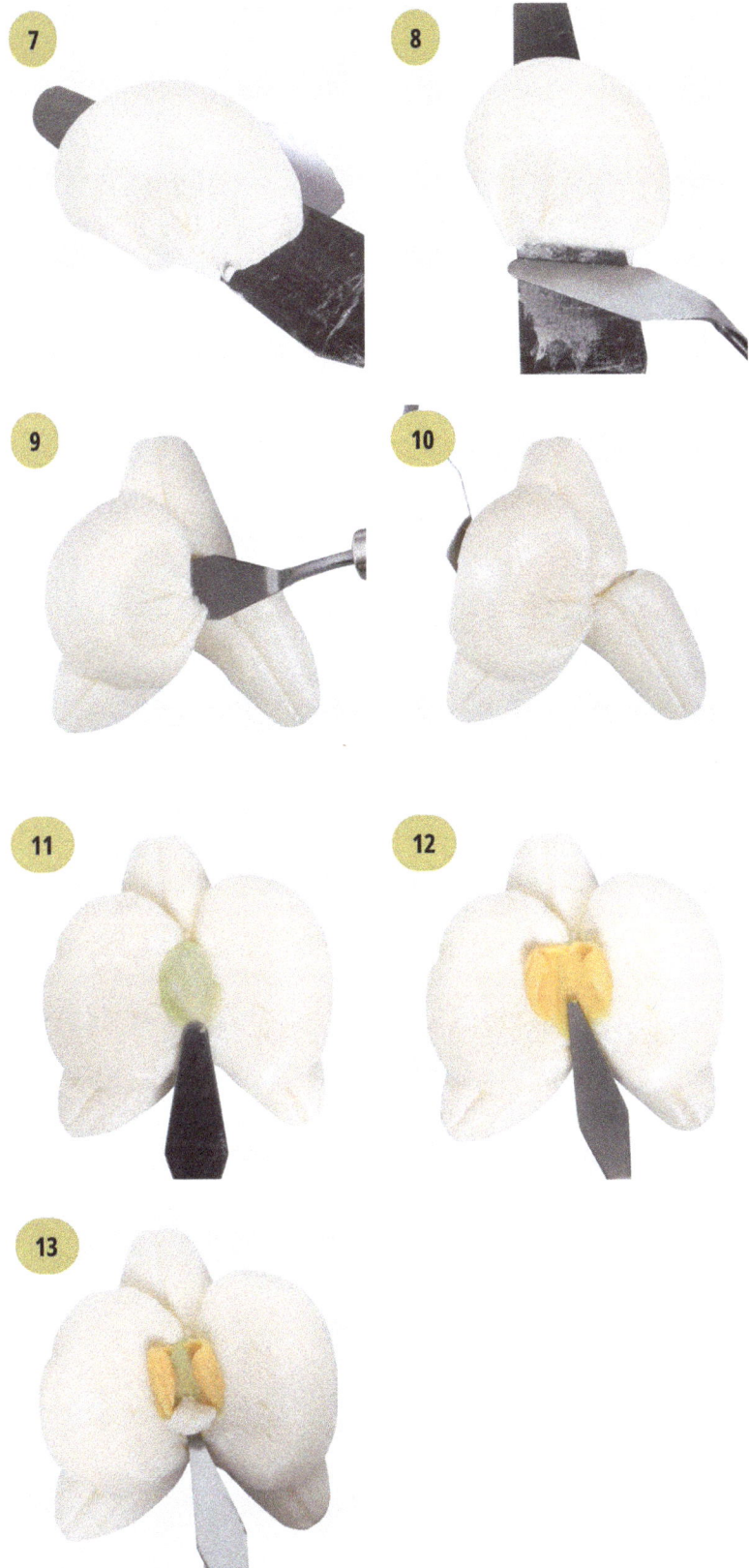

7. In the end, the broad petal should have the thicker, three-dimensional ridge on the outer edge, slightly pinched in the center and should have a wide V shaped bottom.

8. Use a smaller palette knife to cut off the inner edge and bottom of the petal to correct the shape and make things neat.

9. Carefully position the two large, round petals opposite each other in the center of the orchid flower. These lay over the trio of longer petals and meet vertically in the middle.

10. Use a small palette knife to gently lift or reposition the petals for a more realistic look then repeat the process to create the opposite side petal.

11. Smear a small quantity of light green buttercream frosting in the center of the flower. This will also hide the seam between the two round petals.

12. Use a small, pointed palette knife to create the yellow pollinia where the flower's pollen accumulates. This is done with the standard rigid curve petal technique. Leave a curled, three-dimensional edge for a more natural look.

13. Finally, make the small, white anther cap in between the bottom edges of the yellow pollinia. This is simply the same rigid cut petal just way smaller and positioned with the smooth side up.

Iris

The iris flower is renowned for its stunning and captivating beauty. Its allure lies in a combination of its unique structural features and an array of vibrant colors. The intricate detailing of iris flowers is a testament to nature's craftsmanship.

Two-stroke Petal - Style 2

1. To create the bud, start by spreading buttercream in a thin layer over the board in your desired color. Use rigid cut petal technique and a pointed-tip palette knife to create the most realistic shape petal for the bud.

2. Go from left to right to form a right-side petal with the curve on the outer edge. Switch the knife around for the left-side petal. The position of the knife blade matters as well. To create the appropriate shape with the bulk of the buttercream at the bottom as seen in the picture, collect the frosting with the lower portion of the blade and leave the tip mostly clear with just a few scrapes of the frosting.

3. Press and slide the knife so the thicker, curled edge of the petal remains three-dimensional. Ensure that the frosting does not curl over too much and attach to the other side of the palette knife.

4. Add another set of short petals to the center of the bud shape. This creates support on the inside to hold up the outer petals for a more sculptural design.

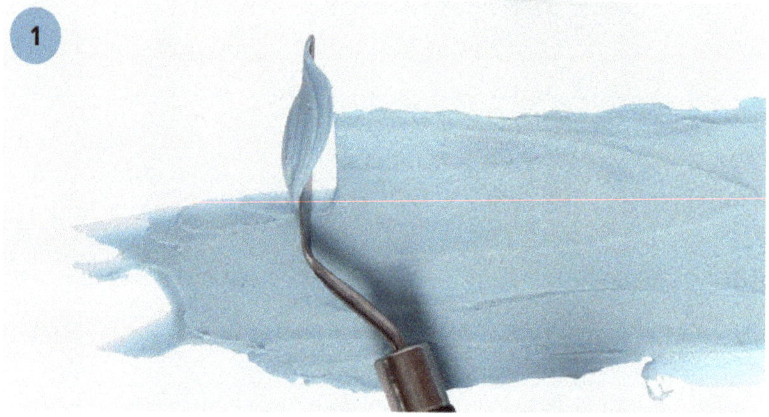

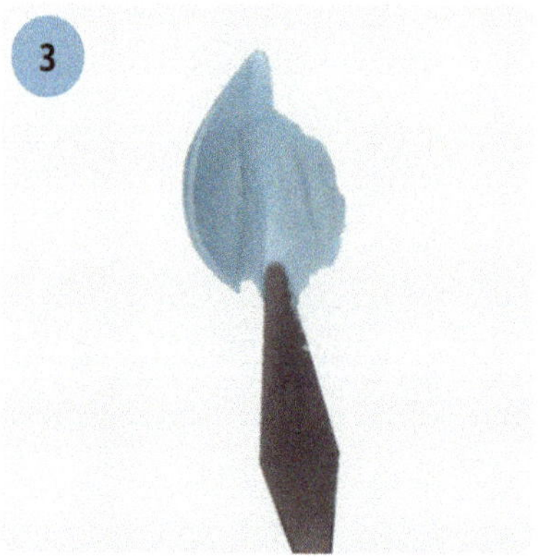

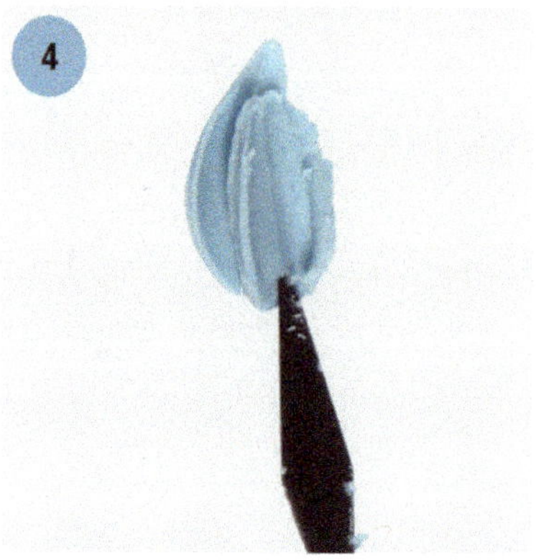

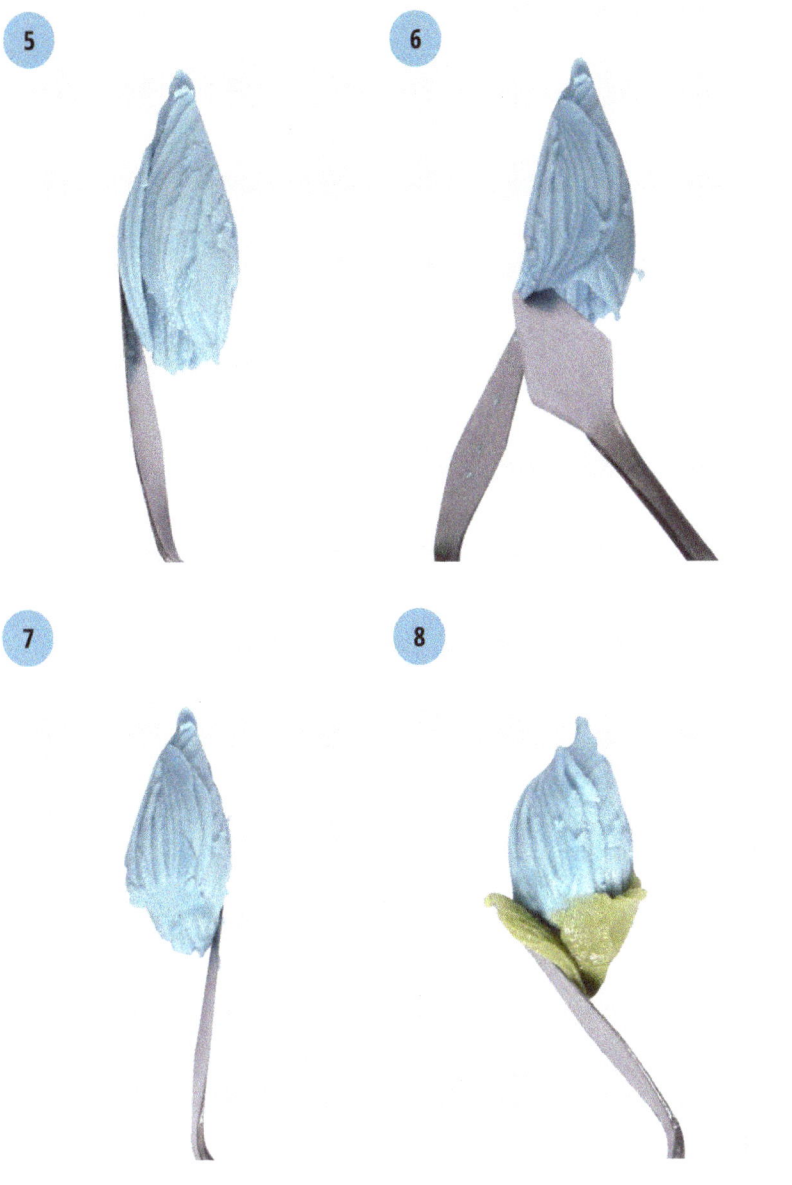

5. Create the left and right petals and affix them to the bud. Use your palette knife to curve the edges over each other near the front center. This gives you a realistic furled bud structure.

6. Add a slightly shorter petal on top of the curved side petals to finish the iris bud shape. This should overlap the center seam with the same smooth or ridged texture of the other buttercream petals you created.

7. Use a clean palette knife to cut off any excess frosting and perfect the shape. Also, trim the bottom of the bud so it is a neat V shape.

8. Make two small green petal shapes for the sepals for the iris bud using the same technique. Attach them to either side of the base carefully with the smooth side out and the ridged, texture side hidden or it could also be the other way around.

Carefully observe reference images of irises. Pay close attention to the different elements, such as the shape, color variations, texture and highlights. Take inspiration from the intricate details of the iris buds, such as the ruffled edges of the petals and the delicate veining.

Start with the base color, in this case, the blue colour and gradually add darker and lighter shades to create depth and realism. You can also use a variety of colors, including whites, greens, blues, and grays, to capture the complexity of the iris's coloration.

1. For the larger top iris petals, repeat the same process with a larger quantity of buttercream frosting. Use a medium length palette knife for this part. Create the ridged texture and allow the petals to curve over themselves further than with the bud.

2. Arrange the right, center, then left petals in a trio as shown in the picture. Use your palette knife to carefully push the petal curve into a pleasing design.

3. For the bottom, dark blue petals, use the same process by spreading the frosting down onto the work board, but this time, smooth side up.

4. Cut the opposite edges of each pair of petals. These two together will create one bell-shaped iris petal. (see 3D Orchid; two-stroke petal)

5. Insert and slide a large pelette a palette knife under each petal and bring them together to form a single petal. They should instantly stick together. However, if the petals have crusted, run a small palette knife or a brush in the middle to join them.

6

6. Arrange each matching pair of dark blue petals on the bottom of the 3D iris flower with the curved edges facing outward. Use the tip of the palette knife to gently lift and curve the bottom edges to create a more natural, sculptural look.

7. Lay down the right petal, then the left, and finally the one in the center. Be careful not to squish them together and avoid flattening the curved edges as you work.

8. Create bright yellow beards for the iris next. Make three small-sided petals using a narrow palette knife. Cut these into small triangles and attach them to the center of each petal using a toothpick.

7

8

Use a toothpick or a cocktail stick to lightly sketch the basic outline of the iris onto the canvas. This will help you with the placement of the flower elements and maintain proportions.

Focus on one petal at a time, building up the layers of paint to create volume and form. You may also use different palette knife techniques to capture the unique textures of each petal.

3D - IRIS | 133

Floral Reverie

Design a garden of buttercream frosting with the techniques you learned in the 3D sculpture flower instructions earlier in this book. With these palette knife techniques, you can create a stunning decorated cake that is as beautiful as it is delicious.

You will need

Tools:
- palette knife
- piping bags
- toothpick

Cake:
- Top tier: Round cake, 15cm (6in) X 10cm (4in) high
- Middle tier: Round cake, 20cm (8in) X 15cm (6in) high
- Bottom tier: Round cake, 25cm (10in) X 10cm (4in) high

Buttercream:
- 1.4kg (50oz) light caramel for crumb coating and final cover
- 100gms (3.5oz) dark green
- 100gms (3.5oz) light green
- 100gms (3.5oz) white
- 100gms (3.5oz) light blue
- 100gms (3.5oz) dark blue
- 100gms (3.5oz) violet
- 100gms (3.5oz) light pink
- 100gms (3.5oz) dark pink
- 100gms (3.5oz) yellow
- 60gms (2.1oz) dark brown
- 60gms (2.1oz) dark caramel

PRO TIP:

Sculpture palette knife painting techniques are much more difficult than other methods. This is especially challenging if you attempt to do it on the side of the finished cake. Practice on a flat surface multiple times first. Also, you can construct the flowers on a board, freeze them for 5-10minutes and then carefully transfer them to the cake.

If the buttercream on the surface of the cake has already crusted, it will be even harder to attach the flowers. Work quickly before the frosting loses its sticky or tacky surface.

A preferred option is to use ganache or a soft-type buttercream frosting that does not form a crust. This gives you much more time to create and attach any sculptured elements done with a crusting type of buttercream or ganache.

FLORAL REVERIE | 135

1. Use a very long palette knife and the instructions for a two-stroke petal or pointy petal - style 2 to form the tall leaves on the top tier of the cake. Use a toothpick to add leaf veins and texture.

2. Create the delicate buds next. This cake example uses slightly marbled blue and purple buttercream frosting for the buds and the petals of the flowers themselves. Use a dry paintbrush to make the transition from stem to sepals seamless.

3. Apply the majestic iris flowers over the top of the leaves and bud stems. Use a clean paintbrush to smooth out any tiny gaps or places where the buttercream does not blend together smoothly. This is especially important for the yellow beards.

4. Add brilliant white orchids next. This includes a couple of green buds off to one side. These are a combination of pale green and white with a darker green piped stem. You can use a toothpick to add the veins.

5. SThe pink lotus buds come next. These should be larger than the iris buds created in Step 1, but the same technique is used.

6. Then, the lotus flowers are applied to the bottom of the middle tier. Position these so they face away from each other. Smooth the space between them with a narrow palette knife. Apply light green coloured leaves as well. Follow the same instructions in creating the iris leaves. Decide if you want to add veins.

FLORAL REVERIE | 136

7. Use a seamless piping bag to draw a guide stem for the leaf stems on the lower tier of the cake. Then, add a few dark green leaves on either side of this branch.

8. Place two sculptural hydrangea clumps. Leave a space in the middle for the peony flower that will come later. This is shown with a white buttercream mound in the images. Use a seamless piping bag to create the small, green center dots on each flower.

9. Position a few white dogwood blossoms to the piped stem so that the leaves stick out on the sides. The number may vary based on the design layout you created. Push through a light green buttercream in a sieve/sifter and position small dabs of buttercream on the center of each flower (see 2D Dogwood flower) then re-pipe the stem with a piping bag to make it slightly thicker.

10. Create the peony atop the white mound of frosting. This helps fill in the angle between the two cake tiers and makes the peony more prominent.

11. Use a palette knife to adjust petals or any other elements of the cake to make a more attractive, natural look.

12. Use a tiny-tip piping bag for the brown edges on the petal divots.

FLORAL REVERIE | 137

Templates

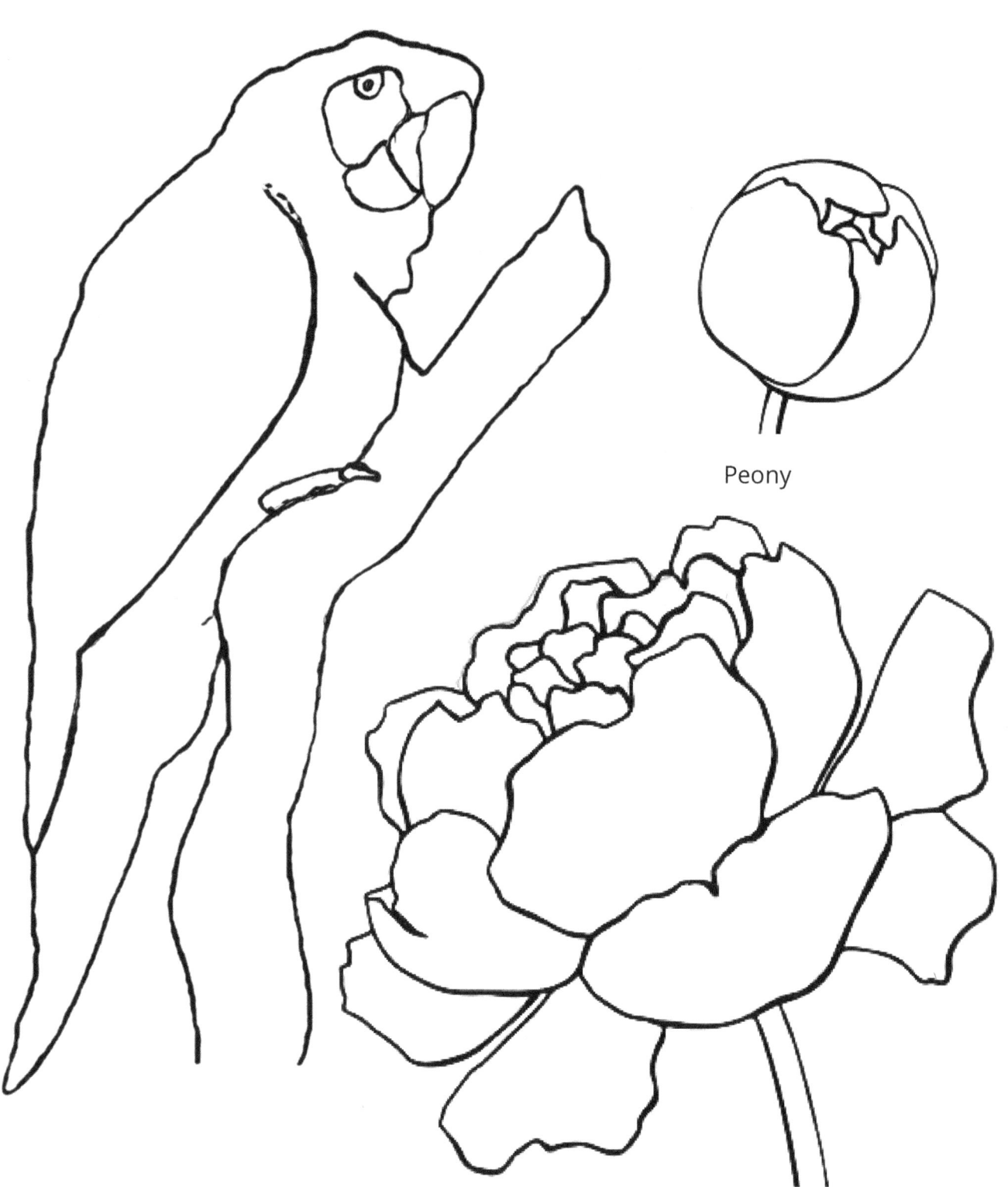

Peony

TEMPLATES | 138

Templates

About the Authors

Best friends Valeri Valeriano and Christina Ong had their eureka moment in buttercream decorating in 2011, in a small kitchen equipped with an oven the size of a toaster. With knowledge gleaned from a YouTube tutorial and armed only with a zip lock bag, they discovered a hidden talent and a passion so vibrant that it has taken their lives in an entirely new direction - and all over the world.

The Queens of Buttercream developed techniques such as lace design, crochet effect, flower piping and, of course, palette knife painting techniques, with which they elevated buttercream decoration to a whole new level. They now teach classes throughout Europe, the United States, Asia, the Middle East and Australia. With their success, the duo has vowed to spread their buttercream knowledge in the indefatigable manner with which they do everything else as they share their recipes, techniques, tips and secrets they continuously innovate in order to deliver the very best to their students, readers and clients. Featured in popular magazines and television shows in the UK and internationally, they have also showcased their talents in four previous bestselling books, The Contemporary Buttercream Bible (2014), 100 Buttercream Flowers (2015), Buttercream One-tier Wonders (2016) and Buttercream Flowers For All Seasons (2018), all translated and offered in many languages.

To find out more, visit www.queenofheartscouturecakes.com or www.facebook.com/QueenofHeartsCoutureCakes or www.instagram.com/QueenofHeartsCoutureCakes

Acknowledgements

We have been designing unique buttercream cake masterpieces for more than a decade now, and yet the excitement to do another creation never fades. In fact, it even multiplies every single time. True to what the closest to us will often say, "These ladies, literally have buttercream running through their veins." And we couldn't agree more.

With every bit of success that we hold in our hands, we would like to thank our ever-loyal friends and followers, you will always have our hearts. Thank you for staying with us all this time. And to those who have just recently joined us in our buttercream adventure, it doesn't matter if you weren't here from the beginning, what matters is you are here, and we will all keep on growing together. This book would never have come to be if not for all of you.

To those who helped us remotely from conceptualising this book, to executing every single project, thank you. The unlimited encouragement, the help in filling the words when we can't find any, the technical support and everything else in between to bring this passion project to life, we are incredibly grateful. Ate Portia and Kuya Ernie, thank you for all the lovely photos and for your patience. We enjoyed all our late night photoshoot sessions.

To our families back in the Philippines, this fifth book and all the books we have written and will write in the future are all for you. We love you dearly.

Index

A
Anthurium, 86, 109
Astilbe, 77

B
Background
    Fun floral dots, 46, 47
    Geometric tiles, 34, 35
    Gold leaf marble, 38, 39
    Marvellous mountains, 36, 37
    Pretty patches, 40, 41
    Scenic landscape, 42, 43
    Soft florals, 32, 33
    Sunrise over the ocean, 44, 45
    Sweet stipple, 30, 31
Basic strokes, 20-23, 26, 79-81, 83, 85, 88, 92, 94-97, 101, 102, 104
    Piping bag method, 20
    Press & curve, 21, 22
    Press & curve with rigid movement, 22
    Press & Slide, 21
    Side stroke, 23, 87-89, 101-105, 122
Bountiful blooms, 110, 111
Buttercream Recipes,
    Bean Paste buttercream, 11
    Italian Meringue buttercream, 10
    QOHC buttercream, 8
    Swiss meringue buttercream, 10-12, 31
    White chocolate Ganache, 12

C
Cake basics, 4, 14
    Colouring, 7, 12
    Crumb coating, 16, 17, 30, 32, 34, 36, 38, 40, 42, 44, 46, 48, 50, 52, 56, 58, 62, 66, 106, 108, 110, 112, 134
    Marbling, 18, 19
        Blended style, 18
        Textured style, 19
    Smoothing, 8, 9, 17, 35
    Stacking and Dowelling, 14, 15
Cakes recipes
    Chocolate cake, 13
    Vanilla cake, 13
Camellia, 88, 89, 113
Craspedia, 77

D
Dahlia, 98, 109
Daisy, 85
Dogwood, 82, 107, 120, 121
Drumstick Allium, 77

E
Equipment, 6
Essentials
    Colour palette, 7, 28, 39, 40, 48
    Composition, 27, 85, 121
    Consistency, 7-10, 12, 24, 31, 33
    Design use, 27
    Layering & detailing, 25
    Understanding angles, 25
    Use of Palette knives, 24

F
Fillers & wild flowers, 77
Floral reverie, 134-137
Floral symphony, 108, 109
Freesia, 83, 112, 113
Fuchsia, 100, 107

G
Gardenia, 90, 112, 113
Gypsophilia, 77

H
Hydrangea, 24, 80, 112, 113, 122, 123
    Rounded petal, 122

I
Impasto technique, 114
Impressionist style art
    Freehand Fleurs, 56, 57
    Fresh fruit basket, 62-65
    Mysterious maiden, 66, 67
    Scarlet the parrot, 70, 71, 73
    Shades of Fall, 58-60
Iris, 95, 106, 107, 130-133, 136

J
Jasmine, 79, 109

L
Leaves & ferns, 76
Lavender, 48, 78, 108, 109
Lotus, 94, 110, 111, 118, 119, 136
Lupine, 77

M
Marigold, 96, 108, 109

O
Orchid, 92, 110, 111, 128, 129, 132, 136
    Two-stroke petal, 128, 130, 132, 136

P
Pansy, 84, 107
Peony, 101, 124-127, 137
    Rigid cut petal, 124, 129, 130
Poppy, 87

R
Ranunculus, 47, 104, 105, 110, 111
Rose, 102, 103
Rose soiree, 112

S
Scabious, 97, 110, 111
Summer garden, 101, 106, 107
Sunflower, 93, 94, 106, 107, 116, 117

T
Templates, 138, 139
Tiles
    Exquisite tiles, 48, 49, 68
    Groovy shells, 52, 53
    Stunning spades, 26, 50, 51
Thistle, 77
Tulip, 91, 111

V
Vegetable fat, 8-10
Veronica, 77
Violet, 81, 112, 113

W
Wax flower, 77

Z
Zinnia, 99, 108, 109

ONLINE BUTTERCREAM ACADEMY

Lifetime
ONE-TIME FEE MEMBERSHIP

ACCESS TO 85 PREMIUM BUTTERCREAM VIDEO TUTORIALS
FOREVER

£139.99 / $175 / ₱9000

10 % DISCOUNT
Use Code: **BOOK5SPECIAL**

www.queenofheartscouturecakes.com

Buttercream Palette Knife Painting Techniques
-A Comprehensive Guide to Textured Art Using Buttercream Icing

Copyright © 2023 Valeri Valeriano & Christina Ong

Valeri Valeriano and Christina Ong have asserted their right to be identified as authors of this work in accordance with the Copyright, Designs and Patents Act, 1988.

All rights reserved. No part of this publication may be reproduced in any form or by any means, electronic or mechanical, by photocopying, recording or otherwise, without prior permission in writing from the publisher.

Readers are permitted to reproduce any of the patterns or designs in this book for their personal use and without the prior permission of the publisher. However, the designs in this book are copyright and must not be reproduced for resale.

The authors have made every effort to ensure that all the instructions in the book are accurate and safe, and therefore cannot accept liability for any resulting injury. damage or loss to persons or property, however it may arise.

Names of manufacturers and product ranges are provided for the information of readers, with no intention to infringe copyright or trademarks.

A catalogue record for this book is available from the British Library.

To request permissions, contact the publisher at
info@queenofheartscouturecakes.com / www.queenofheartscouturecakes.com

Paperback: 978-1-3999-6709-9

First published in the UK, USA and Philippines in 2023

Editing, Cover art and Layout by Valeri Valeriano & Christina Ong
Photography by Ernie & Portia Delgado (Ernie Delgado Photography)

Queen of Hearts Couture Cakes Ltd.
London, United Kingdom UB8 3SG

Milton Keynes UK
Ingram Content Group UK Ltd.
UKHW051841220124
436458UK00001B/2